Raise Your Hand:

Adventures of an American Springsteen Fan in Europe

Caryn Rose

till victory press

Published worldwide by Till Victory Press

tillvictorypress.com | editor@tillvictorypress.com

ISBN: 978-0-9835029-3-7

Cover design by Derek Murphy of Creativindie Covers

Cover photograph by Caryn Rose

September 2012

Acknowledgments

A giant hello and thank you to everyone I met along the way in Europe, but special thanks for camaraderie on the road goes out to Sarah, Beverly, Marci and Howie, and Hanne and Lisa who helped guard the rail in Hyde Park.

Enormous gratitude goes out to my early readers: Alan, Emma, Erin, Lisa and Judy.

Alyssa Archer deserves combat pay for agreeing to edit a second manuscript. Thank you for your deft yet firm touch.

Thank you to Dave Marsh for still caring enough about my writing to edit me, 30 years after we first met.

Thank you to Chris Phillips for publishing me in *Backstreets* for the past 10 years. His guidance and candor has made me a better writer.

Last but not least, thank you to Glenn Radecki. My in-house archivist, my collaborator and partner-in-crime, the maintainer of my master show spreadsheet. Thank you for getting up at 3 a.m. to buy tickets when I couldn't. Thank you for solidarity and companionship and for making me laugh at 2 in the morning, especially when I think I can't possibly write another word.

* * *

Bonus material, including photographs and video, can be found on the web at jukeboxgraduate.com/springsteen and on Facebook at facebook.com/carynlrose.

* * *

Author's Note: Some of the content of this book has been previously published or referenced in some form as part of content on jukeboxgraduate.com, on Backstreets.com, on Twitter or on Facebook. The concert reviews have been edited from their previously published forms for quality and repetition.

TABLE OF CONTENTS

Chapter 1: The Plan

Saturday, 14 July 2012

The alarm went off at 4:50 a.m. The dull grey sky barely illuminated the wet streets, and the air was chilly and damp as we left the hotel. Silently, we walked through the empty sidewalks of the Paddington neighborhood of London on our way to Hyde Park.

Trying to be prepared for the day ahead, I wore multiple layers of clothing and a bright pink L.L. Bean rain jacket. On my feet were wool socks and the most ridiculous rain boots imaginable, emblazoned with the design of the British flag, purchased in a panic upon our arrival in London.

We reached the entrance to Hard Rock Calling at 6:02 a.m. I stood in line as my first name was written down on the list and the person in charge wrote the number 137 on the back of my right hand in thick, black magic marker. The gates would open at 12 noon, and Bruce Springsteen and the E Street Band were scheduled to go onstage at 7:00 p.m., 11 hours from now.

We spread out black plastic garbage bags as protection against the muddy ground and sat down, splaying our flamboyant footwear against the dark, saturated grass. Staring at the boots glowing on top of the green, I started whistling "God Save The Queen" until Glenn, my companion, realized what I was doing and elbowed me to stop.

I pulled my sweatshirt hood up over my head, carefully leaned back against the chain link fence, and closed my eyes. Maybe I would be able to get in a quick nap before the next check-in. Maybe I would stop thinking about how tired I was. Maybe we had a good enough number to get a spot on the front rail. Maybe those dark clouds in the distance would blow through.

The fence rattled behind my head as the next arrivals sat down and tried to get comfortable.

* * *

18 days, five countries, and seven concerts: this was how I spent my summer vacation, running from Paris to Prague to Vienna to London to Dublin, following Bruce Springsteen and the E Street Band around Europe.

While living in New York City provides me with no shortage of opportunities to see Springsteen perform live—I had already seen him seven times since April—for years I have read about the European Bruce fans, and heard about the legendary shows overseas. This element came to many fans' awareness for the first time in 1987 from Dave Marsh's book *Glory Days*.

Marsh discussed how how playing in Europe on the tour for *The River* had a huge impact on Springsteen, and described the European audiences and their reaction to Bruce's music. He pointed out how they were quieter, more respectful, and responded in a way that did not happen in the States (and usually didn't happen in Europe, except at Springsteen shows).

And then there is that legendary Neal Preston photograph of Springsteen onstage at Wembley Stadium July 4, 1985. I'm sure you've seen it: It looks like Bruce is perched on the edge of the world, holding out his microphone towards the gigantic sweeping expanse of Wembley Stadium behind him. It seems like every single person in the place has their hands in the air and are screaming at the top of their lungs.

That photo helped cement my desire to travel to Europe to see live music, period. I remember watching the audience in the Clash documentary *Rude Boy* and feeling the energy crackle through the screen. The audience response to Queen at Live Aid demonstrated that this wasn't limited to punk bands or small venues. The tangible enthusiasm was an amazing thing to me, because it was something I felt was often missing from shows I attended in the States. I wondered what it would be like to be standing in a crowd who were visibly excited and engaged in the performance onstage. It felt more participatory, more powerful, more *rock and roll.*

I would eventually get myself over to Europe for concerts, seeing R.E.M. and Pete Townshend and U2 and Pearl Jam and other smaller, lesser-known bands in Paris and London and Barcelona and other European cities. Every time, I would think that the fans were great and fun and interesting, and the participation undeniably livelier. But I would also think that the fans themselves were pretty much just like me and my friends back home.

The prevailing legend of the superiority of the European audience continued in the case of Springsteen fans, and has only grown as the years have passed. The internet has helped with that immeasurably, facilitating the easy access to information and recordings of shows. The 2003 *Live In Barcelona* DVD, and its loud and frenetic audience brought the notion to more mainstream consciousness; compare the energy in front of the stage in Barcelona to the loud but mostly stationary crowd in 2001's *Live In New York City* DVD. The Barcelona audience barely stops moving for an instant, and it's clear from the expression on his face that Bruce loves every second of it.

Another motivating factor is the growing inattention of American audiences at live rock performances. It seems like there is constant talking during songs no matter where you sit or stand. Requesting that people keep it down, or halt their conversation for the course of one song is rarely received well. You pray that you are able to stand during a show, and not bullied to sit down by everyone behind you, many of whom are chatting or looking at their phones or eating a bucket of popcorn. And then there are the interminable exoduses in and out of your row and up and down the aisle for beer and nachos during slow and quiet songs, no matter how compelling or intense the performance might be.

This behavior is not unique to Springsteen or any other big-name artist, nor is it confined to arenas and stadiums; I've witnessed it at tiny clubs. I do not expect total reverent silence, and it's not like I never utter a sound during a concert. The people I'm talking about are the ones who are behaving as though the band performing is recorded music playing in the background at a party. I have overheard conversations about mowing the lawn, about what medications their doctor has them on, how their boss blew a sale, or any number of inane discussions that could take place before, after or anywhere else besides *during* "Drive All Night," "Wild Billy's Circus Story," "Racing In The Street," or "Meeting Across The River." (And in case you were wondering, those are not arbitrary examples.)

Was a Springsteen show in Europe that different? Were European fans that much better? It was time to find out for myself.

* * *

I have been a Springsteen fan since I was 11 years old, when I discovered "Born To Run" playing on the radio, and thought it was one of the most amazing songs I had ever heard. I would sit with my red Panasonic cassette tape recorder in front of the speaker, waiting for the songs I liked to be played so I could record them and play them whenever I wanted to. I recorded "Born To Run" five times in a row so I could listen to it as much as possible.

My first Bruce concert was at the New Haven Coliseum in 1978. I heard a commercial on WPLR, the local Connecticut radio station, and when I was downtown on a Saturday, I walked up to the Ticketron and asked them if they had any tickets for Bruce Springsteen in New Haven. Never having done this before, I didn't realize that this would be interpreted as a request to purchase one. When the blue-jean, bearded clerk with the John Lennon glasses punched out a ticket and slid it across the counter to me, saying "It's $7.50," I panicked. I was positive he was going to tell me the concert was sold out. But I had several weeks' babysitting cash tucked into my front pocket, earmarked for record albums, so I bought the ticket—and then realized how far away New Haven was from Stamford, especially to a teenager who didn't have her driver's license yet.

I decided to come clean and explain to my mother that I bought the ticket without realizing I was buying a ticket. She looked at the ticket, and glanced at the calendar.

"Fine," she said. "I'll drive you to New Haven."

Mom would later say that had she known what this permissiveness was going to start, she never would have agreed to let me go to the concert. She thought she was doing the right thing because I had told her the truth, and because she thought I would get it out of my system and never do anything like that again.

(I always felt kind of guilty about that, later.)

* * *

I am not going to try to assert that I am the biggest and best Bruce Springsteen fan in the world, because I am not. He is someone whose music I have written about since I was 15 years old, and whose music has always been there, no matter what else I was listening to at the time. I do not think there is anyone else like him, and believe that what he does is a dying art. I believe that when he leaves this planet and the E Street Band are no more, that there will be nothing like them ever again. I found Springsteen's music at the time I was just starting to put together the pieces that connected soul and rhythm and blues and rock and roll to each other, when my love of literature caused me to read anything and everything so I appreciated good storytelling. But he is not the only artist I care about, and not the only music I listen to.

I hate the inevitable, "So how many shows have you seen?" question. I hate the idea of show count as a measure of fandom, and as a result, I don't like to talk about how many shows I have been to. When I meet someone who has seen Bruce Springsteen 500 times, all I can think is how boring that is and how they must not like anything else. So I am not going to talk about my show count, because it doesn't mean much except giving me a larger basis of comparison than someone who sees him once per tour.

I will also tell you that I do not believe that every Bruce Springsteen concert is The Best Concert In The History Of The World. I have never regretted being at a show, but believe that there are performances that are stronger than others. I believe that fandom allows for critical thinking, and I enjoy debate and discussion. This tends to make me a minority and/or a heretic, depending on who you ask. I grew up in a tradition of intelligent rock criticism and enjoy hearing differing opinions on music. "Everything Bruce does is always great" just shuts down any chance to learn or appreciate another perspective.

So I didn't go to Europe to see Bruce Springsteen because I was trying to prove that I was some kind of super-fan. I went to Europe because it was going to be fun, because it was going to be an adventure, because it would give me a chance to visit or re-visit some of the great cities of the world, because I think that travel is important. I also went to Europe because I wanted to kick the tires on all those theories about the superiority of European fans and because I wanted to see what it was like to watch an artist so incredibly American play those songs so far away from home.

And to be honest, I wanted to see Springsteen as much as I could on this tour, because right now we are two men down, and no one knows what is going to happen tomorrow. On the Reunion tour in 1999-2000, I remember the panicky feeling of not being able to get to more shows and *what if this is it?* On the *Rising* tour, I remember sitting at home in Seattle (where I was living at the time) and kicking myself for not getting on a plane and heading East for all of those rehearsals at Convention Hall and that week of madness in Asbury Park as the band geared up to go out on tour. After *Rising*, I think we all calmed down a little and realized that Bruce and E Street were going to be doing this for a while. There wasn't the pressing need to see every concert you possibly could, because there would be another chance soon enough.

And then we lost Danny.

And then we lost Clarence.

We are missing two of nine, and those first shows in the States felt like a spirit walk: Bruce trying to figure out what the show was going to be and how he was going to bring it every night up there without Clarence. He was pushing himself in performance further and harder than he has in recent years, at least to my mind. I thought *Wrecking Ball* was the best Springsteen record since *Tunnel of Love*, and loved how much of the new material was being performed. I usually wait until the band has been on tour for a while before seeing shows, giving them some time to work out the kinks, but this band was solid right out of the gate.

I thought a 17-piece band was just the tiniest bit excessive and wondered how he would make it work, but he did. It was fascinating, watching the live performance grow and morph, watching Steve Van Zandt take more of a role, coming to terms with Jake Clemons finding his place, there was a lot to think about and process and deal with and learn how to embrace. Old songs were different. New songs were good, and amazing in some cases. The half-dozen or so shows I saw in the U.S. made it very clear that this tour was not a tour to sit on the sidelines.

* * *

When planning the trip, our main objective was to see the maximum amount of shows in the minimum amount of time off work, and spend money, time and travel judiciously—while also taking venue and city reputation into consideration. For example, although the audiences (and shows) in Spain are legendary, and we love the country, the initial four-show run kicking off the tour included an expensive flight to the Canary Islands, and then there was a week off between Barcelona and the next gig in Frankfurt. This made that segment of the tour less attractive because it wasn't cost efficient.

We passed every stretch of dates through the same kind of filter, combining the results with how interested we were in a particular country, as well as consideration of what the fans and the queues would be like. I'd love to return to Italy and see Bruce there, but I didn't think I could sleep in the street for three days and then have the energy to survive the show in Milan, no matter how infamous the San Siro audience might be. The Scandinavian countries are lovely and their shows also have quite a well-deserved reputation, but so do their week-long queues in advance of the concerts.

In the end, we decided on a routing that gave us two arena shows in Paris (one on the 4th of July!), Prague, Vienna, London and then two shows in Dublin: this seven-show run was a good mix of shows, cities we loved, cities we hadn't been to, time to sightsee, languages we spoke or could manage well enough in, cities with histories of memorable shows, and easy travel between everything. It was at the midpoint of the tour, so the band would be warmed up. Once we were happy with our itinerary, it was time to start planning in earnest.

* * *

The number one question I was asked about this trip was how we afforded it. We are not independently wealthy, nor did we win the lottery. In 2007, we made a decision that going to Europe to see Springsteen was something we needed to do, and started saving. We had hoped to make the trip in 2009, but circumstances didn't allow it. After the Big Man passed, there was no question that we were going over on the next tour, whenever that was.

We generally prioritize experiences over possessions, so that's where a lot of our discretionary income goes anyway. We cut corners, we pinched pennies. We brought our lunches to work, we went to fewer concerts and did not renew our baseball ticket plan. It's not like I'm any kind of personal finance expert; it was honestly as simple as, "If I want to do X, I can't do Y, so stop doing Y."

The aspect that helped the most was collecting airline miles and hotel points. There are many ways to do this, and there are plenty of resources out there far more knowledgable on this account than I am. Airline miles cut the cost of our flight overseas, our hotels in London and Vienna were free, and the flights to Paris and London were almost free. There's a lot of reading and research to find the best deals, but it was absolutely worth it to help stretch the budget out further.

The rest of the planning was simply a matter of logistics. Compared to when I first started backpacking around Europe, I found planning foreign travel to be ridiculously easy; almost everything could be found on the internet. We bought relevant chapters of various *Lonely Planet* guides, relied heavily on Google Maps and Google Street View, and consulted a wide range of travel websites. We used Google Street View to check out the areas around hotels and venues, so we could see what the neighborhood was like. We also definitely used it to familiarize ourselves with the area around venues. (In some ways, it felt like cheating.)

Additionally, fans on the various Springsteen online forums offered advice and insight on their individual cities, especially on how to get to and from venues that weren't in the center of town. Like all travel advice, many times this information was correct and helpful; other times it wasn't and we had to wing it. This is all part of the fun of travel.

We chose hotels based on location, price, proximity to public transportation and/or the venue, the neighborhood around the hotel, overall quality and whether or not they had free wifi. Every property we considered had a website with at least a few pages in English. We absolutely could have stayed in bare-bones accommodation—some people even camp while on tour, bringing expenses down even further—but that was where we drew a line; this was still supposed to be an actual vacation. While we didn't need to stay at five-star hotels, we needed some level of creature comfort.

Finally, buying tickets to shows overseas is the simplest thing of all. All of the ticket agencies had English language e-commerce pages (if not full mirror sites) so there was no need to get friends in those countries to diagram out the transaction screens with translations, like I did in 2000 when I was buying tickets for Pearl Jam in Portugal and Spain. The adventure was getting accurate information about ticket on-sale times since some dates went on sale without an official announcement from the Springsteen camp, as well as getting up at (or staying up until) 3 a.m. almost every day for an entire week to buy the tickets at 9 or 10 a.m. European time. There was a little bit of panic and excitement and worry, but for all intents and purposes, it was exactly like buying tickets for shows in the States.

* * *

And, after all of that, after buying rain jackets and new sneakers and universal sink stoppers and plug converters, after eight months of planning, I got on a plane and headed for Paris.

Chapter 2: Paris

Tuesday, 3 July 2012

All trains travel to Paris, the signboard said. This seemed clear enough, so we wheeled our suitcases onto the RER (the Paris regional rail), found a place to sit, and took a deep breath.

We had flown all night from JFK to Heathrow, and then grabbed the connection to Charles De Gaulle. And now, incredibly, here we were, on our way to see Bruce Springsteen and the E Street Band at the Palais Omnisports de Paris Bercy. In some ways, it didn't feel all that much different than flying to Buffalo or Atlanta or Kansas City, except for the not inconsequential fact of *being in Paris*.

Two hours later, after checking into the hotel and unpacking a little, we headed for the venue. Emerging from the Metro, the first thing I saw was a guy wearing a hat and a shirt from Asbury Park's Stone Pony club. Chuckling to myself, and just wanting to save some time, I walked over and asked, "Hey, where's the GA line?" The second-to-last thing I expected was a look of panic and not-understanding and the heavily-accented, halting English saying, "It is at Gate 27." (After three weeks in Europe and witnessing the overwhelming amount of Stone Pony merchandise in the possession of fans there, I understood why I once saw the club's owner driving a Rolls Royce.)

The last thing I expected was right outside Gate 27. Walking around, looking for whoever had the line—wait, no, *queue*—sign-up sheet, we finally found someone to point us in the right direction. We were standing in front of the dude with the baseball hat and the clipboard, waiting our turn, when suddenly a familar face looked up and said, "Hey there!"

Instead of the line being run by some guy from France or some woman from the Continent, it was being run by Ted, from New Jersey. We see Ted at every Bruce show in the States, no matter where it is. He proudly informs us that he started the line on Saturday, getting there ahead of the French fans.

Plus ça change, plus c'est la même chose.

* * *

Paris always overwhelms me, that mix of history and culture, the tourists and the monuments and the art. I can't walk three feet without wanting to stop and stare. I emerge from the Metro and want to take pictures of everything I see: statues, parks, people, stores, posters for the shows, ads for *Wrecking Ball*, the boulevard outside our hotel window. It is not the first time in Paris for either of us, but I think Paris is always magical.

During the winter, I had downloaded a podcast called "Coffee Break French," about 20 lessons' worth, just enough to bring back whatever French I might still possess out of the dusty recesses of my brain. (I would joke that no French course would teach me the phrases I really needed to know, like "*Ou est l'file d'attente d'admission generale?*" ["Where is the GA line?"] or "Please put your sign down.") It turned out to be enough to let us operate outside of the "ugly tourist" radar; random people in shops or the Metro would talk to me in French first. We stayed on the other side of the river not far from the venue, away from all the tourist craziness and in more of an actual neighborhood. It was nice to feel like you were part of the rhythm of a city instead of just barreling through it. And we discovered that we were not the only people in our hotel in Paris to see Bruce Springsteen, but we would be the only non-French people doing so.

We knew there would not be a lot of time to sightsee, with only one non-show day available to us. But still, all things considered, we saw everything on our list. We climbed up to the top of the Arc de Triomphe and skirted around the Eiffel Tower. We saw the Musée Rodin and the Louvre, walked down the Champs Élysées and strolled along the Left Bank.

We ate *steak frite* and *entrecote* and *croissant* and *sandwich au jambon.* There was a lot of *sandwich au jambon,* to tell you the truth. You would think a ham sandwich would not that be that exciting or that delicious, but let me assure you that in Paris, it is both of those things. There was one day that out of necessity we ended up eating *sandwich au jambon* for breakfast, lunch and dinner, and it never got boring. The bread is amazing, the ham is tasty, and the combination is fabulous.

The queue to get into the arena in Paris was the same shuffling mess of any line anywhere in the world. It felt different because people were smoking everywhere and drinking beer openly and, of course, speaking French. There was a sandwich vendor walking up and down the line, the sandwiches wrapped in paper in a cloth-lined box hanging around the vendor's neck, like an old-fashioned popcorn vendor. Women selling earplugs walked down the line with their trays, looking like cigarette girls. (They actually had three different types of earplugs for sale and had many buyers.)

You didn't need to know any French to know what the security guards were yelling: *keep moving, let's move please, you're in the wrong line.* I got my ticket scanned, held my arms up and my purse open as I went through security. "C'est tout?" ["That's all?"] he asked me, and I nodded; this is the whole reason I carry a small bag into shows. Once I was past those formalities I was on auto-pilot, heart beating just a little faster as we scurried down the stairs and through the passageway and onto the floor. Left or right? I pick a side and walk briskly towards the entrance to the pit at the front of the stage, holding my wrist up for the security guard to see my wristband, just like I would in Seattle or St. Louis or Philadelphia.

We sat down on the floor, just like everybody else was doing, holding their signs and their water and their snacks (you could bring your own food in), and settled in for the duration. You wait for the light operators to go up the ladders, you wait for the instrument techs to go through their final paces. You wait for the crowd around you to start standing up, and then wait for the initial rush as everyone re-jockeys into place. You wait for Bruce's water and Gatorade and sponge to be prepared, you wait for the setlists to be brought out on the stage, you wait for the camera operators to take their place. It is the same ritual that you have been through before, which is comforting, but you know you are not in Kansas any more.

An arena is an arena anywhere in the world, and if you've been to enough concerts in arenas, you will feel right at home no matter where you are. Bercy is an older venue, built in the early '80s. On the inside, it could be anywhere in the States. There is nothing measurably different: the barriers, the plastic seats, the flashing advertisements, the cinderblocks, the vendors taking the bottle caps off of your water, the inequity of women's bathrooms vs. men's bathrooms. In Paris, when the line for the ladies' got too long, groups of two or three women would huddle together and walk into the men's toilet with impunity, and no one looked askance. (I did something similar at the old Spectrum in Philadelphia during the *Tunnel of Love* tour and had security guards threatening to call the cops.)

Once the lights go down, it is even more familiar, and yet so different.

* * *

Palais Omnisports de Paris Bercy, 4 July 2012

Setlist: We Take Care of Our Own, Wrecking Ball, Badlands, Death to My Hometown, My City of Ruins, Spirit in the Night, The E Street Shuffle, 4th of July, Asbury Park (Sandy), Jack of All Trades, Because the Night, Darkness on the Edge of Town, Johnny 99, Darlington County, Easy Money, Waitin' on a Sunny Day, The Promised Land, Apollo Medley, Independence Day (solo piano), The River, The Rising, Out in the Street, Land of Hope and Dreams

Encore: We Are Alive, Born in the U.S.A., Born to Run, Bobby Jean, Dancing in the Dark, Tenth Avenue Freeze-out, American Land

Cherche place. That's what the Parisian scalpers write on the signs they hold as they walk around, so they don't have to expend energy with the French version of "Who's got tickets?" or "Anyone selling?" The GA line is familiar: the homemade t-shirts, the couples wearing matching shirts, the one dude wearing his flag bandanna so proudly you can't even bring yourself to make fun of him. It could have been any Springsteen show anywhere.

It could have been, but it was in Paris on the 4th of July, one of the few arena shows in Europe this summer. Expectations were running high. Expectations started running high the minute the show was booked for July 4th and the minute that the city was Paris. There is endless precedent for these expectations, given Bruce's history of shows on that date and shows in that city.

It was not a particularly hot day, but there had been three power outages at Bercy (one of which we were inside for), and they were so worried about a fourth that Antoine de Caunes (a well-known French television presenter and enormous Springsteen fan) came out to explain the situation and ask that, if for some reason the power should go out again, that we all stay calmly in our seats. This probably explains why there was no sign of any air conditioning for the entire show, causing the entire band to become drenched in sweat, for Stevie to be continually gesturing for water for the band, and towards the end of the set, for Bruce to be hand-carrying cups of his water and blue Gatorade to the fans around the front platform.

This is the kind of adversity the E Street Band could potentially thrive on. Instead, it felt like the poor conditions resulted in a show which was an uneven mix of strong performances combined with some lackluster ones. This also could have just been a symptom of the first concert after a break, or the fact that the show is in need of some revision at this point in the tour.

The good: "Spirit In The Night," "E Street Shuffle" (an audible called as the result of a sign request), "Darkness on the Edge of Town," even the sometimes over-played "Darlington County" was enjoyable, not least for the date-appropriate lyric. The crowd especially loved "Because The Night" even if it was one of the weaker versions I've seen in terms of a lack of overall propulsion and energy, but I will, again, attribute that to heat. Maybe it was just because it was the 4th of July, but "Born In The USA" sounded muscular and fantastic, the complete opposite of the album version, Garry's bass rippling through the arena.

The outstanding: "The River," which had an extraordinarily loud singalong; Bruce stopped and let the audience sing the next two lines, before taking the song back, and then the crowd picked up the instrumental refrain again once the song had ended. It was powerful and haunting and the best kind of Springsteen live experience. And, of course, solo piano "Independence Day," Bruce at the piano in the blue spotlight, singing with power and pathos. It was magnificent, and alone worth the price of admission. Part of Springsteen's mastery is how he can embody the material each and every time and make it utterly believable and compelling.

The surprising: I will confess that I generally find "4th of July, Asbury Park (Sandy)" overrated and at times, overwrought with significance. It was expected tonight, given the date, but watching it thousands of miles away from home, in front of people who have never been to Asbury Park or New Jersey made it seem different, seem special, feel magical. "Land of Hope and Dreams" felt tight and sharp without too many "People Get Ready" refrains. "Tenth Avenue" and the video tribute to Clarence still breaks my heart, even though I have seen it half a dozen times; I am fairly sure it will always break my heart.

What needs some help: "My City of Ruins" is feeling bloated. Bruce gave some of the speech he gave in the US, and translated some of it into French after the English. But then that segued into a call-and-response of "Are you ready for a houseparty?"after telling us that this was "a song for the things that leave us and that will always stay with us." He then tried to bring it around by saying "When you throw a party, you know who's there and who's not." I think that probably happened because he was worried that the crowd didn't understand him, and was trying to get a vocal response, but I also think that it would be okay at this point to either drop this particular number from the set, or not use it for the "roll call" and remembrance of Danny and Clarence.

"Rocky Ground" needs to come back, it is just as important (if not more so) than "Jack of All Trades" or "Easy Money" (back in the set tonight since Patti was present). I am pleased to see that the new material has not been summarily abandoned by this point in the tour, especially in the midst of the stadium run. Tonight is the first time I felt that I understood "Wrecking Ball" sufficiently; I have always liked it musically, but hated the lyrics. I'm still not sure I'm in love with them, but the point is that it introduces the theme of the evening with the "tonight, all the dead are here" line. (And, it remains a brilliant contribution from the horn section.) "We Are Alive" works, commanding an attention and a spirit that is one of those "only in Europe" instances; the crowd sits patiently through the story that introduces the song, so there is no vacuum created by mass loss of attention; they meet him vocally in the refrain, singing it back each time. It is what I always hoped would happen with this song.

I feel like the Apollo Medley could be traded in for "Sweet Soul Music" or "Shake" or something, anything else that could easily accomplish the same purpose of paying tribute to the band's musical heritage and showcasing the expanded E Street lineup. "The Promised Land" suffers from the same placement after "Waiting On A Sunny Day" that it has all tour; it is trivialized and weakened in that spot, and should be given a rest or a new home.

Finally, the sad lack of songs from *The Promise*, a record that almost no one has heard songs from performed live, will continue to be troubling. There are two signs in my suitcase (which we just plain forgot tonight in our excitement) that will try to make our case on this front from now until Dublin, and judging by other signs I saw in the audience tonight, we are not the only ones that feel this way.

The encore still feels excessive to me, with too many greatest hits making it feel bottom-heavy. The reappearance of the utterly unnecessary "American Land," a song that always feels fake and forced, does not help mitigate that impression. It is an encore that works better in a large stadium, capturing the attention of the casual fans and the people at the very top, than in the intimacy of an arena where the audience is—by proximity alone—more engaged.

The crowd was wonderful, boisterous and dancing and jumping all over the arena. There were signs everywhere, there were flags from a dozen different countries, the songs were sung in every accent you could imagine. The audience was loud and when they weren't, they stood still and listened. Adele and Pamela Springsteen were present, sitting in the front row stage left, on their feet for almost every song. (Some Italians near us started cheering Bruce's mother with the "Badlands" refrain as she walked onto the floor and was escorted to her seat.)

The heat, I fear, was the worst culprit tonight, sapping the crowd's energy towards the end (Bruce saying that the Paris crowd had "a lot of heart" despite the temperature) and impacting the band's as well, based on sweatier-than-usual appearances and occasional pained expressions. But it was still wonderful to stand in that crowd tonight, and I look forward to night two tomorrow.

* * *

Palais Omnisports de Paris Bercy, 5 July 2012

Setlist: The Ties That Bind, No Surrender, Two Hearts, Downbound Train, Candy's Room, Something in the Night, We Take Care of Our Own, Wrecking Ball, Death to My Hometown, My City of Ruins, Spirit in the Night, Incident on 57th Street, Because the Night, She's the One, Working on the Highway, I'm Goin' Down, Easy Money, Waitin' on a Sunny Day, Apollo Medley, For You (solo piano), Racing in the Street, The Rising, Out in the Street, Land of Hope and Dreams

Encore: We Are Alive, Thunder Road, Born to Run, Glory Days, Seven Nights to Rock, Dancing in the Dark, Tenth Avenue Freeze-out

Who could have known what the second night in Paris was going to be like? There was a setlist, which apparently got tossed to the wayside rapidly as Bruce called audible after audible, hitting the right notes. The result was a collection of songs that worked, that wasn't just a jukebox or a greatest hits machine, that wasn't pandering to the crowd (a crowd which, by the way, did not need pandering to. They were eating out of his hand from the first note). There was amazing energy on the floor, in the pit, in the very top rows of the venue, people standing up with their arms up in the air for almost every song. I was standing about eight rows back from the barrier between Stevie and Patti, and was surrounded by Germans, Parisians, and a whole host of Scandinavians. The dude who looked like he might be trouble, wearing the faux biker colors and LAS VEGAS baseball cap, turned out to be the dude jumping up and down excited for "Easy Money" and who knew "Seven Nights To Rock" by heart. You were happy for the 20-something German girls who had a "Glory Days" sign. You held a water bottle for the guy from Norway trying to take a picture of Bruce at the piano with his iPhone.

After years of standing in apathetic American crowds, where, on more than one occasion I have been mocked for my enthusiasm, it was like a homecoming to stand among unabashed Bruce geeks of every nationality who didn't care what you looked like or what you sang or how loud you sang it or how badly you danced. Parisians had zero trouble jumping around like crazy fools, waving their arms in the air, or clapping along on cue. There was the need for a couple of looks of death tonight at conversations in various languages during quieter songs, and there were some questionable signs (and questionable sign etiquette; "Racing In The Street" is not the time to hold up your sign for a minute and a half), but this crowd was, once again, in it for every second of every song.

This crowd sang everything. Every refrain, every line, every possible melody or refrain they could sing back to Bruce, they did. We started singing the "whoa-oh-oh" counterpoint during 'Dancing In The Dark' and were the only people doing it for about 10 seconds until everyone around us picked it up (and I'm pretty sure that originated in Europe). They sang back the melody of the refrain on "Downbound Train" and "We Take Care of Our Own" and the *whoa*'s in the choruses in both "Something In The Night" and "Death To My Hometown." They sang it back in the right places, not trying to excessively prolong the song like they did the night before. The crowd participation lifted the energy, instead of interfering with the pace and flow of the show, which happened a few times on Tuesday night.

"Candy's Room" into "Something In The Night" was the first clue that this night would be off the charts. The Europeans sing "Candy's Room" with as much heart and soul as we do; they stop dead still and let "Something" sink into their bones, eyes closed. Crisp and focused, it was the best "Something" I have ever heard, and not just because I did not have to pray that no one would talk or have to ask someone to shut up. It was the best "Something" I have ever heard because it seemed like Bruce felt he had something to prove.

I dislike the need to attempt to engage the crowd at the start of "Spirit In The Night" by adding a gospel-tinged dramatic intro—the crowd doesn't need it, they know and love "Spirit" and will be fine once you actually start singing it, Bruce—is what I want to tell him, even if it is perhaps an attempt to continue the soul music theme through the show, it starts to feel like just too much. However, it was an off-the-charts version of "Spirit," loose and energetic. Bruce crawled down the front runway like something out of the *Creature From the Black Lagoon*, inserting himself into the sea of hands and cameraphones at the end. Then he headed to the back of the stage to serenade the fans sitting behind the stage, before grabbing Jake Clemons to go on a little adventure down the front of one of the other runways.

I am one of those fans who did not (and do not) like Jake having any of Clarence's stage business besides his saxophone playing (and he has truly improved greatly, playing stronger and with more confidence), but tonight it was fine and even great because it wasn't something Bruce would have done with Clarence, it was this crazy free jazz exploration with just him and the sax at the end of that platform, and it was true to the song and it was something new and it fit perfectly. It was so much fun to watch.

"Incident On 57th Street" overwhelmed me, so much emotion and energy and heat and a little bit of hurting feet. Who would have expected this now, at this show, at this point in the setlist? But these were all songs that there had been signs for, repeatedly. (There were a lot of signs. There were a lot of good signs. Okay, there are also signs requesting to dance with Bruce for Dancing In The Dark and there were signs for "Glory Days' and "No Surrender" but there were also signs for "Chimes of Freedom" and "Ain't Good Enough For You" and "Backstreets".)
"Incident" was brilliant and beautiful and raw. Standing in Paris, listening to a song set in Spanish Harlem, featuring characters that always felt as classically New York City as the Empire State Building, you realize that it doesn't matter who the characters are

or where they might be, all that matters is the story and the melody and it's no wonder that anyone, anywhere wouldn't be transported by it.

"Because the Night" into "She's The One" was a steamroller, a powerhouse, it was dark and sexy and hard and strong and yes, all of that, all of that was there. The solos were sinewy, lithe, powerful. Nils was off the charts. Bruce was playing in a different, other space, a less safe space, a good space. They were what they were supposed to be, how they should feel like—not that it was 1978 because it's not 1978, but the emotions still exist, you know? They are still there, just different.

And aside from the rarities, even the crowd-pleasers were wonderful. "Glory Days" was outstanding, and I cannot remember ever having so much fun singing along. It was not stale, it was not boring. "Working On The Highway" had Bruce in full *Louisiana Hayride* Elvis mode, enhanced when someone handed up a glittery cowboy hat, which Bruce gleefully donned and then vamped his way through the rest of the song. When he was done, he turned around and shook his ass just like Elvis, all the way back to the main mic.

There was a lot of ass shaking tonight. There were a lot of Bruce & Patti moments. There was a lot of Stevie and Bruce love. There was a lot of E Street tonight, you know? They played hard, they played solid, they played strong. I think they always probably try to do all of those things but it sometimes just doesn't work. Tonight it did.

I thought "I'm Goin' Down" was going to be "Rockin All Over The World" because Bruce stood there hitting the same guitar chord five or six times until the band regrouped and realized what they were going to be playing next. This version of the song was better than any full-album *USA* show "I'm Goin' Down," or any random U.S. sighting. But then again, the entire performance tonight was absolutely fantastic. The band was pumped. The audience was on fire. The two of them fed each other back and forth and back and forth and just when you thought things were going to stop, they would heat up again.

"For You," with Bruce on solo piano into "Racing In The Street"? You didn't see that coming. No one saw that coming. I'm not even sure Bruce knew what he was going to play next until he finished one song and decided what the next one was going to be.

"Waiting On A Sunny Day" (or "Waiting," as the Europeans call it), was still "Sunny Day," the part of the set I dread and despise for its utter banality. There are so many songs the audience can sing along to (and already do), so many other potential candidates for a song during which Bruce can make a point about family (especially since the children pulled up to sing are performing party tricks and not actually fans of his music). The child who did get pulled onstage to sing didn't know more than the three lines, and definitely didn't want to go running around the stage with Bruce.

Who expects to get choked up during "Thunder Road" after all of these years? I always love it and never get tired of it, but tonight became something larger, or rather, re-inhabited the *gravitas* it should rightly always possess. The emotional element for me was the universality of it all, the Scandinavian fellow with his arm in the air during the "It's a town full of losers" line, the four women in the seats swaying back and forth arm in arm, the energy and the emotion rushing behind you and up onto the stage and out back again. And then, immediately after, it is "Born To Run" making perfect sense thousands of miles away from the New Jersey Turnpike.

"Seven Nights To Rock" was a great surprise, and even more surprising was how everyone knew it—American audiences are flummoxed by this one more often than not. Maybe most fans couldn't list Jane and Lorraine and Nancy Lee and Betty Lou, but hell, I get them mixed up too, but that didn't stop the crowd from dancing and waving their arms and smiling as big as you could possibly smile. And then, and then, Bruce goes over to the keyboard, and starts playing the keyboard with his head (when this happened at another show, I did not believe the reports at first) and then he went over to the mic stand, flipped the guitar around, and started playing the guitar against the mic stand with his butt. Patti had looks of disbelief and amusement. Stevie couldn't stop laughing. Garry and Roy were also smiling more than usual tonight; hell, everyone on that stage was smiling. The horn section were up there doing their little dances.

And at the end—at the very end, the end of "Tenth Avenue," when we wanted one more (we kept checking the time, wondering if Bruce was going to try to break his own record), but knew there was no way anyone up there could give us one more, and it was already 12:30, he stood there, hitting his fist to his heart and pointing at the crowd. (At one point at the end of the set—this is hard to explain, but it was as though the crowd were applauding each other, looking up and down and around and applauding something that was not the band, but rather the energy in the venue, applauding their part in the show.)

It was the biggest, loudest party ever, it was E Street past and E Street present, it was as authentically Bruce Springsteen as you could ever get, even if it was thousands of miles away from the homeland.

* * *

There is a row of restaurants and shops and bars across from Bercy and, each night after the show, Glenn would bolt across the street once we emerged from the venue to get ahead of the rush. We would buy water (lots of water, thanks to the absence of air conditioning in the arena) and Orangina and Gini (a French soda he loved from previous visits) and given the choice between tuna and ham, came back to the hotel each night carrying—you guessed it—*sandwich au jambon*. We picnicked in the hotel room while writing up the report for *Backstreets*. We have both been writing for both the magazine and the web site for almost 10 years now, and just like after Springsteen shows in the U.S., we ran back to the hotel to file reports and reviews.

We sat on the floor or on the bed eating *sandwich*, typing away, cursing the hotel wifi which did not like Tumblr or YouTube or Flickr. It was not glamorous, but it was delicious, cheap and fun.

The second night (when we once again sprinted for *sandwich au jambon*, getting the last sandwiches in the cooler) we were flying on adrenaline and euphoria at the end of that tremendous show. Once we were finished writing, we couldn't fall asleep, and stayed up talking to friends in the States on Twitter and listening to the Mets game via the internet. We were awake until we started to hear the birds chirping, and finally fell asleep just as Paris started to turn grey with sunrise.

We had one whole day to ourselves in Paris, where we walked through the streets as much as possible, looking at everything and soaking up the atmosphere. We had lunch in Montmartre, lit a candle for my mother in Notre Dame, bought a book at Shakespeare & Co., and navigated the hordes at the Louvre. On our final morning, the women at the *patisserie* where we got *pain au chocolate* and *petit brioche* each morning greeted us like we were regular customers, and the clerk at the corner market where we bought drinks and snacks waved as we walked by, saying, "Bonjour, Madame." With more than a little regret, we hopped back on the RER to Charles de Gaulle, and headed for Prague.

Chapter 3: Prague

Saturday, 6 July 2012

Following Paris, the Springsteen tour went on to Denmark and Zurich. We had no desire to see Bruce as one of many acts at the Roskilde Festival, and skipped Zurich in favor of heading to Prague, a place that neither of us had been and were excited to visit.

Prague had originally been chosen as a good midpoint between the shows in Paris and Vienna. It was only after we had made most of our arrangements that a date was added in the capitol of the Czech Republic. How convenient! It would mean cutting a day from our time in Vienna, but it gave us an extra show without any additional travel.

We arrived in Prague via EasyJet (the European equivalent of Southwest Airlines) late on Saturday afternoon. The show was on Wednesday, and we thought this would give us enough time to see the city and spend some time queuing for the concert. Prague was extraordinarily beautiful, small, and manageable. Although we paid attention to what was happening in Denmark and Switzerland, the next two days were decidedly detached from Bruce Springsteen.

We got to spend time being tourists, visiting Prague Castle, the Jewish Quarter, the Astronomical Clock, and the sites of the Velvet Revolution. It was a lovely, fascinating city, where just walking around random side streets was highly enjoyable, so we did a lot of that. We had a book called *Eat Goulash and Enjoy Beer in Prague Like A Local* whose premise was to help tourists who spoke zero Czech learn just enough in order find their way to non-tourist restaurants, where the food and beer would be better and/or cheaper. (If you learn nothing else, beer is *pivo*, and is cheaper than water everywhere in Prague.) The challenge was a lot of fun, but after five days of the meat-and-carb heavy Czech cuisine I was desperate for a fresh green vegetable of any kind.

Early Monday evening, we had just gotten back to the hotel when Glenn opened up his laptop and said, "Wow, someone here says there's already 10 people in the queue for Prague."

We looked at each other for two seconds before putting on our shoes back on and heading out.

The original plan was to head down to the arena around noon on Tuesday, the day before the show, and see what was going on with the queue. With there being a date in Zurich on Monday, and the practicalities of travel time between the two points, we didn't think anyone would start lining up too early. We wanted to get a low number for this show and had budgeted the extra days in Prague accordingly, so we could queue and make all the check-ins without worrying we wouldn't get to see the city.

The ride to the venue via tram took 25 anxious minutes. Why didn't we just go check things out Monday morning? Why was the tram going so slowly? How many people would arrive before we did? When we (finally) arrived at the Synot Tip (it's a sports betting firm) Arena, we walked around nervously for a few minutes until we saw a sign directing us to the GA queue at Gate 2. To our relief, only one person had showed up before we did, and we got numbers 12 and 13.

I have to confess that after our numbers were written on our hands, I went around the corner where no one could see me, and jumped up and down a few times in excitement. Short of some kind of terrible mishap, we were going to have very good spots for the concert.

* * *

If you don't already know, the GA process in Europe is different than it is in the U.S. and Canada (and if you do, skip the next few paragraphs). Anywhere from a week to a few days before the show, a fan (or group of fans) decides to start the queue in a given city by showing up at or near the venue with a tent and a sleeping bag. They post signs around the venue directing people to their location, and as other fans show up, they put their name on a list and get a number written in magic marker on their hand. The number represents your place in the queue.

In order to prevent a situation where hundreds of people are camping out in a commercial or residential area for up to a week before the concert, and the associated liability issues, the queue runs on the basis of check-ins every few hours. This means you can leave and come back; someone stays put the entire time (hence the tent and the sleeping bag) so there is always someone there to sign people up.

You have to show up at every roll call and acknowledge your name on the list, or you lose your spot. The check-ins generally run every 3-4 hours until 11 or midnight, and pick up again early in the morning. Most venues or promoters know how this works by now, and many respect the process. Springsteen management tries to help out, and after some mishaps earlier in the tour, were very involved in the queues we were in.

When everything works correctly, the fans who have been there the longest get into the venue first and get the best spots. When it doesn't work (as, for example, the fans at the Manchester, UK show will tell you), it means that people who just showed up a few hours before the gates open get in front of people who may have been waiting there for days on end.

I realize how insane this all sounds to someone on the outside, and this is why the North American shows now have a lottery-based process for general admission. However, I have had terrible, terrible luck with the lottery over the past few tours, to the point where I no longer even try at important shows, because I cannot take the disappointment of always being stuck at the back of the floor. The first-come, first-serve system was a big factor on the plus side of going to see shows in Europe.

No matter where you are in the world, there is always going to be someone who is willing to sell their grandmother for a front row spot at a Bruce Springsteen concert. There are still line politics and there is still line corruption. I believe it is a better system than the one in the States, but think that its days are numbered.

* * *

There were seven check-ins on Tuesday, the day before the show: 7 a.m., 10 a.m., 12 p.m., 3 p.m., 6 p.m., 8 p.m. and 11 p.m.

We stuck around when it was only two hours between check-ins since the round trip back to the hotel took an hour. There was a Metro stop not far from the venue, but we traveled by tram because it was closer to our hotel, and stopped in front of the venue. Other fans took taxis to every check-in because it was quicker, and they didn't have to try to figure out the Prague transit system. A one-day transit pass cost a little over $5 for 24 hours, while taxi fare would have been about $30 per ride.

The tram was always on time. It was never early, but it was also never late. We got so used to the ride through the outer neighborhoods of Prague that we could read, nap, play games, write. We saw Prague Castle at sunrise, at midday, at sunset, lit up at night. (I never, ever got tired of looking at it.) I would stare up at the cornices of buildings and churches, looking for hidden architectural gems. I would teach myself more Czech by reading the signs as we passed by. *Náměstí* meant square. *Sady* meant a park. Many street names had familiar words with *"ska"* added to the end, like *Holandska* or *Moskevska.*

From our pre-trip research with Google Street View, we knew that there was a large shopping center across from the arena, with a Tesco Extra (think Super Target) as the anchor store. (We would later find out that there were other stores as well as a food court, public toilets, free wi-fi and mini golf.) There was also a McDonald's on the other side of the arena, but that was about it for amenities nearby. It was a purely residential area with row after row of grey concrete apartment blocks that looked like something out of a Cold War spy movie.

The first fans in the queue had already gone across the street to the Tesco and bought air mattresses and cushions and tarps.

(This was in addition to the tents set up nearby.) When the sun was out, everything turned into an impromptu beach; when it rained, they would fashion a shelter with the various pieces. We made our own trip to Tesco, and bought two camp chairs for around $20. (I was sorry I didn't sign up for the Tesco club card, because we would encounter them again in London, and again in Dublin.) Other fans would arrive, get a number, see the various encampments and either ask us where we got everything or figure it out. Other fans didn't care about creature comforts and instead came back with cases of beer and bags of snacks, leaning against the wall or sprawled out in the parking lot.

* * *

There is a commonly held belief in the fan community that you need to put in your time in the queue and "earn" your spot, and over the two days of waiting, we were subjected to several lectures from other fans about "the spirit of the queue." I do not disagree with the general sentiment, which is why I turned up on Monday and put in my time. I also met a lot of great people in the queue in Prague. But I don't think every Bruce Springsteen fan has to be my friend, nor do I believe that a punitive series of check-ins is the way to achieve camaraderie.

And when you try to declare that the first check-in on the day of the show will be held at 5 a.m., before public transportation starts running, it feels a lot less like "spirit" and a lot more like trying to use the process to improve your friends' (who got high numbers because they arrived after the show in Zurich) position in the queue. (Even Springsteen tour personnel working with the fan queues discouraged early morning check-ins at other shows, although no other queue so far had tried to enforce a 5 a.m. check-in.) This kind of inter-queue politics and plain old bullshit wasn't unique to Prague, nor is it unique to European fans. It is just part of life on tour.

On the other hand, I don't think it's fair for fans to turn up and plead that they should be able to skip check-ins because they'd never been to Prague before (and yes, that happened), but there are very good reasons for the check-in system versus a week of camping out before a show. It only took a couple of hours of a relatively small group of fans arriving and congregating early Tuesday afternoon before someone from the hotel attached to the arena came out and complained, shooing everyone over to the other side of the parking lot.

* * *

By the first check-in at 7 a.m. Wednesday morning (yes, the queue successfully fought and won the battle against that 5 a.m. declaration), the line had grown to several hundred fans from all over Europe. Venue security began to arrive. Vendors set up beer stands and food stands and picnic tables. The local fans started turning up and getting upset that there were already so many people waiting. Given the fact that the guy who ran the springsteen.cz website had been publishing updates regarding the queue every few hours, I did not feel sorry for any of them. Except for one bozo who pushed his way to the front of the line and refused to move (only to be tossed out by security not long before the gate opened), most other concertgoers seemed resigned to the fact that there was a line and they were at the back of it. There were just too many of us already there to try to stage an uprising.

On show day, there are some check-ins in the morning, but after noon or so, you are at the venue for the entire day. We were there for good after the 10 a.m. check-in; we were just too far from the hotel. In most queues, you will see that the first 20-30 people really don't move, even when everyone else disappears between check-ins. If you have a low number, you want to ensure that you get the spot you have waited all that time for. You want to make sure that a rogue line doesn't start, that some local dudes don't turn up and push their way to the front, that the line doesn't get moved to the other side of the stadium, that someone doesn't decide to fake a number, or any one of a number of things that can happen.

There is a lot of waiting, but it is not calm or relaxed enough that you can actually accomplish something (and continual line drama does not help with that). I did manage to grab some tiny naps in in the early part of the day, amazed that I could fall asleep sitting upright in the middle of a parking lot next to a stadium, surrounded by people. But there's not much else you can do besides sit around and talk. You don't have a lot of possessions with you because you obviously don't want to carry much into the show. We knew we were abandoning our camp chairs and donating them to the people of Praha 10. (By the way, thanks for letting us use your free community wifi. It seemed like a fair trade.)

Some time between 4 or 5 p.m., our gate opened up. Security let the line enter the venue in small groups, ten or so at a time. They do it that way in order to try to give everyone a fair chance to get to their spot without it degenerating into a mad, crazed dash for the front. My heart was beating so fast when the line advanced forward, after all of the hours of waiting. We were still at the beginning of the queue, there was no one else inside ahead of us, and yet, still, I was incredibly nervous.

While you wait, someone inevitably asks what your strategy is, what location you are going to try for. My answer is always that it depends on where the people ahead of me decide to go. When I finally made it down the stairs and onto the pitch, the spot we wanted was taken, but there was still somehow room at the end of the front runway. I grabbed that, and Glenn took the place immediately around the corner. Logic dictated that those spots should have already been gone by the time we got in, but the two girls from Spain at the very front of the line ended up choosing the side of the runway because they were worried about the crush from behind.

At every show this tour, Lef, a member of the Springsteen crew, takes two photos from the perspective behind the center microphone. One is when the stage is set up but before the audience is let in, and the other is once the house is full. It was impossible to miss me in the shot taken in Prague, because my smile lit up the entire photo. (My father's response, when I sent him the link to the photo: "You couldn't get any closer?")

It was the best spot I have ever had at a Springsteen show, and I had to travel to the Czech Republic to get it.

Synot Tip Arena, Prague, Czech Republic, 11 July, 2012

Setlist: The Ghost of Tom Joad (solo acoustic), Badlands, Prove It All Night, We Take Care of Our Own, Wrecking Ball, Death to My Hometown, My City of Ruins, Spirit in the Night, Candy's Room, She's the One, This Hard Land, Jack of All Trades, Atlantic City, Because the Night, My Love Will Not Let You Down, Working on the Highway, Shackled and Drawn, Waitin' on a Sunny Day, The River, The Rising, Land of Hope and Dreams

Encore: Thunder Road, Born in the U.S.A., Born to Run, Bobby Jean, Seven Nights to Rock, Dancing in the Dark, Tenth Avenue Freeze-out, Twist and Shout

It is overwhelming to watch a Bruce Springsteen show on the end of the front runway. It is somewhat less intense in an outdoor venue than in an arena because there is more distance from the stage, but it is still very much this sense of "Here is this person I see all the time in photos, and now he is right in front of me, and I am touching his guitar and I am smacking his hand as he walks by and high-fives everyone around him."

The intensity of the sheer proximity takes you back to your first experiences of live music, and you feel younger. You remember when every concert was life or death. It is incredibly exciting to be that close, so close you could reach out and rest a hand on his knee or his boot, so close that you have to move back a little when he comes forward. Anyone who tells you that that spot isn't exciting is 1) lying 2) jaded and 3) should give up their spot to someone else. It is rock and roll. It is electric.

I was so close tonight that it was impossible to take notes and difficult to take photographs. When Bruce Springsteen is standing over you dripping sweat onto your forehead, you aren't thinking 'Gee, I should take my camera out." You are thinking things like "He always looks so much older closer up," and "There are grey hairs in his eyebrows, I don't remember those," and "There are polka dots on the back of his vest, I have never noticed that before?" and "How on earth does he have a t-shirt on under a button-down under a vest and that tie, no wonder he sweats through it instantly." His boots had silver studs on them, and I immediately flash on the relevant line from "Saint In The City."

"Spirit In The Night" began, and Bruce strolled down to the end of the runway like he always does. He was on his knees right in front of us, as everyone around him, male or female, had a hand on an arm or a leg or a shoulder (or other body parts, which I didn't see but heard about later). Though I had previously expressed my dislike for the new extended gospel intro and outro, tonight it was tighter and crisper. I had to admit that it worked and I liked it. I think it was especially successful tonight because Bruce had a very vocal response from the crowd in front and he didn't feel the need to continue to ask for one.

Once again, Jake and Bruce picked up the routine that they started the second night in Paris. They came to the center stairs for the last verse, sitting there, the two of them, and it felt right and fun and proper. Bruce then brought Jake all the way down to the front, but Jake did not look too happy about being so close to everyone, even though everyone behaved nicely. (When he got there, I said something like, "Don't worry, Jake, we won't bite." He didn't look convinced.)

"This Hard Land" (by sign request, from a group of fans from Greece) was immediately perfect for the crowd and the setting, just like the acoustic solo "Ghost of Tom Joad" as the first song also fit beautifully, the context only becoming obvious with the first notes. I loved hearing Bruce talking about hanging out with Vaclev Havel during his first visit on the *Ghost of Tom Joad* tour, and the audience clearly appreciated the mention.

"Atlantic City" was one of those odd but wonderful interludes where you think, "I am singing a song about a town in New Jersey most of these people have never been to and will never go to, thousands of miles away from it," and you truly understand that one of the standout strengths of the song is that it's a good story, told well. The enthusiastic crowd response to "My Love Will Not Let You Down" was one of the reasons that you go to see Bruce Springsteen in Europe, where you become one of the hundreds of people bouncing up and down with their fists raised, singing the words in whatever their particular accent is, but with no doubt at all whatsoever that they completely comprehend the song's meaning.

"Working On The Highway" was super-charged tonight, with extra pelvic thrusts sprinkled throughout, no doubt the result of two sides of the runway being completely female. Someone handed up a "I'M SEXY AND I KNOW IT" sign before the song started; Bruce grabbed it and held it up to the crowd, hamming it up. At the end of the song, a fan handed up a pink cowboy hat. Bruce put it on and modeled it for the crowd, then turned to face the video camera operator so she could put him on the sidestage screens so he could see himself. He mugs, he poses, the crowd laughs and cheers. He says, "This pink hat makes me wanna… makes me wanna *dance*," and vamps back up the runway to the center mic.

I love turning around and watching the audience at key points during the show, especially in a stadium. (Despite the name, the Synot Tip Arena is actually a stadium, albeit a smaller one at 20,000 capacity.) In Prague, I turned around to discover that the audience in the stands was sitting down. The band would play two more songs, and I would turn around again, and they would still be seated. But there is nothing Bruce Springsteen loves more than a challenge, whether it is rain or heat or power failures or people sitting on their hands. He could have played it safe and played a string of known hits, thrown in a "Bobby Jean" or "No Surrender" or "Lonesome Day," and he didn't. He stayed true to his vision of the set, but he never passed up an opportunity to exhort the crowd to stand up. This seemed to have mixed results (this is judging by what was shown on the video screens, since I honestly could not see) as they would stand up but sit down as soon as Bruce went back to the center stage. (Once they reached the encore, "Born In The USA" finally got them up for good.)

Tonight was the first time I got to see the reworked version of "Shackled and Drawn" which brings Cindy Mizelle to the front of the runway with Bruce at the end of the song. It is one of the standout songs from the new record, and I am glad to see Springsteen taking advantage of the expanded E Street Band lineup. Cindy is great, and I wish Bruce could figure out more ways to use the E Street Choir (and wish he would please bring back "Rocky Ground" already).

"The River" remains a big favorite with European audiences, and the audience reaction is tremendous. "Land of Hope and Dreams" gets better every single time I hear it. The arrangement of the new version has gelled so now the band can just focus on playing the heck out of it, and they do, every night.

"Thunder Road" was once again an emotional experience. What hits me in Prague is the same thing that struck me in Paris: the universality of it, singing it with every person around you, of every age and from more countries than you would ever imagine. The performance of "Born In The USA" was stellar, loud and strong, exorcising the years of bad synthesizers right out of it. The crowd loved it. I never sing "Born In The USA" back home because I don't want anyone to think I am one of those people who doesn't understand what it's really about, but it feels different doing it in Europe. Everyone in Europe is singing it because it was an enormous hit and because it's a good song. It is pretty damn liberating to be able to just sing it without worrying about subtext and baggage.

By the time Bruce pulled out 'Seven Nights To Rock," he had broken curfew and I was starting to wonder where I was going to find more energy. "Tenth Avenue Freeze-Out" couldn't feature the walk into the crowd for the Clarence tribute that he had been doing in the arenas, the video clip montage of Clarence, and of Bruce and Clarence, that tells the entire story of their friendship in less than a minute. Instead, Bruce came down to the front of the center platform, standing there holding the microphone high in the air as the video played on the big screen behind him. We yelled CLARENCE and BIG MAN and just cheered it all as loud as possible. Despite having witnessed the video eight times now, I am still enormously moved by it; and watching the video in such close proximity to Bruce just amplifies that feeling. He is out in the audience, standing among us; we are watching him paying tribute to his friend, and he is watching us paying tribute, and we are all bound together in that moment of remembrance.

The encore was hysterical, Bruce asking Stevie and Garry if they know what time it is, and they all go along with the shtick of shaking their heads and pointing to their wrists and *no, Boss, I don't know what time it is*, and then Bruce says, "We can't go home, it's too early," and—of course you knew what it was going to be: "Twist and Shout". You want to go to Europe to dance to "Twist and Shout" in a stadium with European fans, you want to jump and dance, you want to shake your ass with new friends and total strangers. We bumped butts with each other, we waved our hands in the air and generally made complete idiots of ourselves, and I never wanted it to end.

The front of the pit crowd was incredibly international. Particularly visible was an enormous contingent from Poland (who knew my very Polish neighborhood back home in Brooklyn!), the folks from Greece who were at the beginning of the queue, and enough residents of the Tri-State area to have found ourselves in a spirited debate earlier in the day regarding the northernmost Wawa in New Jersey and the quality of the coffee at the 7-11 next to the Windmill in Long Branch. We met some fans from Finland while waiting for the tram (people would get on and hold up their hand with their GA number on it in greeting like some kind of secret sign), and I now know more people from Norway than I have ever met in my entire life.

At the end of it all, you stand there and watch the band leave, and then watch Bruce turn to wave again, and salute the crowd, and then you stand there and shake your head and think, *that just happened.* Then you hug everyone around you and exchange email addresses and find your way out of the stadium, another incredible night for the memory books.

Chapter 4: Vienna

Thursday, 12 July 2012

The main train station in Prague was disappointing in its modernity until we got up onto the platform. Then I had the grand European train station experience that I always remembered, the platforms, the swooping arches of glass and steel. In my imagination, I am wearing a a tailored suit, complete with hat and veil, and am standing next to a set of matching luggage, smoking a cigarette in a long holder.

In actuality, I am wearing sneakers, jeans and a U2 t-shirt stating "boys play rock and roll," and my reverie was broken up by a contingent of Springsteen fans from New York and New Jersey chattering loudly in East Coast accents as they walked down the platform.

I slept a lot of the way from Prague to Vienna, to the disappointment of the French students in our compartment who wanted to teach us a card game. Under normal circumstances I would have been only too delighted to get more practice for my French and let them practice their English, but we had gotten about four hours of sleep after the Prague show, and the show in Vienna was later that night—**and** we had an early morning flight to London the following day. Sleep had become a precious commodity.

The border crossing from the Czech Republic into Austria was first denoted by the text message from our European SIM carrier announcing we were in a new territory, and only next by immigration inspectors. I once again bemoaned the loss of romance in European travel.

By the time we reached our hotel near the Opera, I was starving. I had earlier expressed the opinion that since I was in Vienna for the first time, I wanted *Wiener Schnitzel.* We quickly abandoned that plan as we passed a sausage stand and then a *Konditorei* with decor straight out of the '50s on the way to the hotel. Instead of spending 18 Euro on one main course at a nearby restaurant that looked like any restaurant back home, we backtracked to the sausage stand for several different kind of *Wurst,* picked up cakes at the bakery, and had a picnic in the hotel room. Glenn got to use his German, and I got to have *Currywurst* and *Käsekrainer* (a cheese sausage, which was as amazing as it sounds) and an authentic Viennese pastry. It was all of Vienna we were going to be able to experience before heading to the show, but it felt like a lot.

Ernst Happel Stadion was your typical massive European soccer stadium, sterile steel and concrete. We picked up our tickets—actual hard tickets for the first time this tour, since they didn't have electronic tickets for this show—and headed through the security chutes and through the tunnel onto the pitch. Feet clattering against the terraplas (the plastic tiles they put over the grass so it doesn't get ruined), we made our way to the front pit area. The queue hadn't been in that long and everyone was still sitting down, like they always do, to conserve energy and preserve space and help ensure that the crush builds slowly.

Turning around to take some photos of the expanse of the stadium behind us, I realized that the audience in the stands was so very, very far away, due to the stadium being shaped like an oval and the stage being placed on the long side.

There was a lot of beer in Vienna; there were vendors walking around with large coolers that dispensed draft beer. There were stands with those big Bavarian pretzels and I'm still sorry I didn't have room in my stomach after the sausages to try the cheese pretzel. I am pretty sure those were a million times better than the lukewarm rubbery knot of dough you get at your average U.S. stadium.

We expected to run into Austrian friends (whom we had met at Giants Stadium in 2009) at the show, because we knew they would be there and they had told us on Facebook where they were planning on standing. What we didn't plan on was running into old friends from New York, who had gone from seeing Bruce in Paris to Krakow, and were now in Vienna before heading into the countryside the next day. Lee and Mary have radar for finding us in a Springsteen pit; if we planned to meet up we probably wouldn't have found each other. It was nice to see the familiar faces of old friends so far away from home.

They went to find a place on the side and in the back to watch the show from, while we headed into the crowd. It would be fun to meet some more Austrian Springsteen fans, I thought. Glenn's German was more than serviceable and so there wouldn't be much of a language barrier.

* * *

Ernst Happel Stadion, Vienna, Austria, 12 July 2012

Setlist: We Take Care of Our Own, Wrecking Ball, Badlands, Death to My Hometown, My City of Ruins, Spirit in the Night, Rendezvous, Loose Ends, Empty Sky, Trapped, Jack of All Trades, Because the Night, Darlington County, Working on the Highway, Shackled and Drawn, Waitin' on a Sunny Day, Raise Your Hand, Tougher Than the Rest (solo piano), Racing in the Street, The Rising, Lonesome Day, Land of Hope and Dreams

Encore: We Are Alive, Born in the U.S.A., Born to Run, Hungry Heart, Glory Days, Seven Nights to Rock, Dancing in the Dark, Tenth Avenue Freeze-out, Twist and Shout

The Vienna setlist was the type of set I feared we would get in Prague, given how slowly that show sold and how the audience just sat there for the first few songs. But unlike Prague, where Bruce constructed a powerful setlist and worked that setlist to engage the audience, with a few impromptu touches for the diehard fans, in Vienna the lack of response from the crowd caused him to veer all over the place, and the setlist just fell apart.

It's still a mystery why this show opened with the standard "We Take Care Of Our Own"/ "Wrecking Ball" combo, when every other show since the Isle of Wight got something special to kick it off. However, that wasn't the reason for the lack of enthusasiam. Bruce couldn't even get a response during "Badlands," but instead of just going into something like "Prove It All Night" that people would know, he went into "Death To My Hometown" which people simply did not. "My City Of Ruins" did not connect, at all, and neither did "Spirit In The Night," although every song was played just as well as they've played the songs on any other show, if not better, given how solid the band is at this point of the tour.

We were in the front of stage pit (an area for which premium, more expensive tickets were sold) and yet were surrounded by people who did not seem to know the songs, but yet clapped in

4-4 time along to everything. I had been warned about this phenomenon by European friends; the clapping wasn't enthusiastic, but rather a polite, automatic response that was disconnected from the music.

Conversely, any kind of energetic response on our part was met with odd looks; the few people in the crowd who were clearly big fans and trying to enjoy themselves by dancing or singing along received a similar reception. Even further up towards the front of the stage (we were about 15 - 20 people back) there didn't seem to be the kind of vocal audience reaction you have come to expect at an European show. The crowd was enormously subdued throughout the stadium until the encore.

Although the setlist may have seemed amazing on paper, this show was incredibly uneven. It lacked cohesion, direction or any kind of thematic arc. Sure, I loved hearing "Rendezvous" and could hear "Loose Ends" any night of the week. "Empty Sky" as a sign request might have worked had it been a full band electric version. But a solo acoustic rendition of this number (even introduced as one of Bruce's favorites) did not command the crowd, it just lost them.

The signs were the culprit tonight. There were too many, they were too big, and the fans who brought them did not know when to hold them up and when to put them down. They dominated the view in the front of the stage for the beginning of the show until Bruce went into the crowd and grabbed a handful. That helped get rid of most of them, but not all, like the 15-foot "Tougher Than The Rest" banner that was passed over people's heads and held up in the middle of the crowd for an entire song. (If you think that might have completely blocked the view of the stage for the unfortunate fans behind it, you would be 100% correct.)

I saw Bruce prop the sign for "Trapped" up against his microphone stand and thought, "Oh, good, that will get them going for sure." I was excited and ready for my first European big stadium "Trapped" and got my camera ready and everything, only for—nothing to happen. I turned around and watched the expanse of the stadium bowl, completely filled, do absolutely nothing in response. No arms in the air, no crowd roar, nothing. It fell flat, which I have never seen happen with that song, anywhere, ever.

However, following that up with the solemn and unfamiliar "Jack of All Trades" was asking for failure. I appreciate that Bruce has certain cornerstones of the set and I do not like it when new songs are abandoned mid-tour, but this was not the right choice at this particular time. There were so many directions he could have gone to bring the crowd in before heading back to the new material. He could have gone to material from *Born In The USA* (and given the audience's reaction in the encore, that probably would have helped). He could have tried the "Because The Night" / "She's The One" pairing. He could have taken any number of other approaches, but instead zig zagged all over the place due to the disconnect and the enormous quantity of signs in the crowd. There are many occasions on which Bruce has abandoned the written setlist and revised his plans on the fly to great effect, like the second night in Paris. Vienna was not one of those occasions. The end result was that you felt like you were being energetically jerked around from song to song.

"Darlington County" was the first selection chosen to engage the crowd (after abandoning "Johnny 99," tossing the capo aside) that I actually agreed with. "Sunny Day" was "Sunny Day," and a setlist decision I would have agreed with tonight, except for the girl taking off her shirt on the video screen in front of God and 50,000 Springsteen fans. I understand that there is historical precedent for this tactic in Vienna*, but that doesn't make it right. I expect that behavior at a heavy metal show, not at a

Bruce Springsteen concert. It's alienating and insulting to the other women in the audience (and likely many of the men as well, not to mention the children). This was an unfortunate trend during several songs tonight.

"Raise Your Hand" was lovely and wonderful except for the fact that no one in the audience apparently felt capable of actually raising their hand, until the end of the song when Bruce stood there and begged for it. "Tougher Than The Rest" was prefaced by an introduction mentioning how many signs he had seen requesting the songs, and how puzzling that choice was in this city. It was an absolutely lovely performance, but also seemed to fall flat except for the people clapping along aimlessly.

"Racing In The Street" was a surprising choice, given the inattentiveness of the crowd, but it's such a powerful piece of music that it never fails to command an audience—except in Vienna. When my eyes were closed, everything was perfect. When I opened my eyes, the couple to my left started making out and the couple to my right (the woman wearing a Bruce shirt who kept going up on her boyfriend's shoulders during any remotely lively song) had a vigorous and loud conversation… before starting to make out. Then everyone else around us lit a cigarette during Roy's solo (which was anything but tedious or boring, full of color and shading), resulting in our hasty retreat to the back side of the pit during "The Rising."

The encore was fantastic, getting the crowd onto their feet and finally keeping them there. "Twist and Shout" in a European soccer stadium when everyone is happy and dancing and singing is absolutely incredible. So are "Born In The USA," "Born To Run," "Hungry Heart," "Dancing In The Dark," and "Seven Nights To Rock." All of it flowed, worked, moved, and accomplished everything the main set couldn't.

It was a good show with great moments; there were three tour premieres, and impeccable playing throughout. I mourned the lost opportunities but will never be unhappy to have seen a Bruce Springsteen concert.

—

*At the Vienna show in 2009, a woman wearing a shirt reading "Jersey Girl" took it off and threw it at Bruce, resulting in the only performance of that song in Europe, ever.

* * *

When we later abandoned our spots in the crowd during "The Rising," and headed for the back of the pit, I ruminated on how the crowd in Vienna was nothing like I thought it was going to be. Vienna would end up being the second-drunkest crowd this tour (coming in after Dublin), and it was the crowd that smoked the most. They smoked when they were bored. They smoked when they didn't like the song. They smoked after a song they did like. It was absolutely impossible to escape it, even in the back.

Going from the intimacy of the 17,000 seats in Bercy in Paris, to the smaller stadium in Prague, and then to the 50,000 seats in Vienna, reminded me of how much I usually dislike stadium shows and avoid them at all costs. Even when you are close to the stage, you are still far away. The best seat in the stands is still a considerable distance from the stage; it only took sitting there once, years ago, to realize I would never do that again because of how disconnected I felt from the energy and the performance. When the crowd is paying attention, there is definitely a feeling of excitement and unity that can only happen in such a large audience. But when it's not, a stadium show can be about as calm and dull as watching a movie. The crowd largely sits down, conversations are louder, there's more getting up and down for beer because you are so physically distant from the action on the stage.

The encore was happy and boisterous, hit after hit after hit rolling off the stage, the stadium lit up as bright as day. Glenn and I danced together on the terraplas at the back, watching thousands of Austrians singing and dancing and waving signs and American flags. At the final bow, we scurried out of the stadium and back to the Ubahn, back to the boulevard near the opera, and back to the sausage stand, who was thankfully still open.

Chapter 5: London

Friday, 13 July 2012

I do not remember anything about our 7:30 a.m. flight from Vienna to London, because I was sound asleep before the plane took off. I had finally gotten to bed around 3 a.m., once we had finished eating, repacking, and writing up our report on the Vienna show for *Backstreets.*

I woke up just as we began the descent into Heathrow, and saw sunlight and blue sky. Two seconds later, the pilot remarked that the weather was nice now, but that it was going to rain soon, and my heart sank. The U.K. weather had been the bane of my pre-trip existence. Their summer so far had been brutal, wetter and colder than normal. Everyone kept hoping that it would change but the little grey clouds hanging over England never seemed to disappear from the weather websites, no matter how many times I checked. My rain jacket was adequate, but we weren't talking about a warm summer shower in New Jersey. I didn't know if I was ready to deal with an entire day (and night) of cold, heavy rain like they had at the Manchester show in June.

At Immigration, the official made small talk, asking us about the weather and what we were going to do today. I repeated what we had been told on the plane, adding, "But we're going to go buy Wellies as soon as possible, because we're going to Hyde Park tomorrow," I said.

"Oh, you're going to see Bruce? Yes, you'll need those boots!"

She stamped our passports and sent us on our way.

* * *

I absolutely love London. It was the first foreign city I traveled to as a British Invasion-obsessed 20-something in 1984. I lived there for a few months in the late '80s and I've visited many, many times since then. But I still had that flushed first feeling of excitement as the train pulled into Paddington Station. I was back in the land of so much of the music that I love. I was back in the land of salt and vinegar crisps, amazing Indian food, and chocolate digestive biscuits. I was going to see Bruce Springsteen and the E Street Band in Hyde Park (Hyde Park! The Stones played there, although not in the same location.), and I was more than a little excited. I was in London!

We knew that we didn't have nearly enough time for our liking (and it was Glenn's first trip to London), but finding more time would have meant skipping a show or cutting sightseeing time somewhere else. On top of all of that, by this point we were fighting exhaustion something fierce, and needed to get some rest. The nights had run later than we'd anticipated, and there had been fewer opportunities to catch up on sleep than we'd thought. However, we were also firm in our conviction that we wanted to make an effort to queue for Hyde Park in order get the best spot that we possibly could. It was going to be quite the juggling act, and we honestly had no idea if we would be at all successful.

At some point on Friday we heard that the queue had already started for the first show in Dublin. A lot of fans I had talked to skipped Vienna in order to save their energy for Hyde Park; others skipped both Vienna and London because they wanted a good spot in the queue for Dublin. As we made our way from Abbey Road to the Hammersmith Odeon to the Joe Strummer Subway, I decided that I couldn't think about it too much or my head would explode. We just weren't going to get to Ireland until Monday afternoon, and I had to get through Hyde Park first.

Friday night, we got dressed up and had a lovely, civilized dinner with a good friend at his private club in Soho. Although he is a crazy Springsteen fan like us, it was wonderful to take a break and talk about world events and the Olympics and catch up on each others' lives. It was good to talk with someone who completely understood why we were doing what we were doing, but was also connected to the real world. We got dressed up, ate actual vegetables, drank wine, and forgot about how tired we were for a little while.

The next day brought a world of contrasts as we sat in the mud in Hyde Park, eating our cheap cheese sandwiches from the shop next to the hotel.

* * *

Besides the weather, the other constant subject of discussion in the queues and online over the past few weeks had been the mud situation in Hyde Park. The record rainfall, combined with a regular pace of shows at the concert site had destroyed the grass and created a large mud flat where there used to be lovely expanses of green grass. Photographs of muddy crowds at other shows and news stories in the U.K. press about how the concert site was being viewed as a health hazard were hot topics among fans. I had been prepared to sacrifice my show sneakers to the mud god of Hyde Park and either buy replacements or just manage for the rest of the trip. Glenn's show shoes were a sturdy pair of Doc Martens.

But everyone we had met along the tour who had been at the show in Manchester kept urging us to consider buying Wellington boots (the Brits call them "Wellies")—solid, knee-high rubber boots. Our new friend Sarah explained that in Manchester, the difference between the people whose lips were blue and the people who were wet and cold but not freezing were the ones who were wearing boots.

We decided to buy boots as soon as we got to London.

The question was, of course, where would we find boots? Or rather, where would we find them easily and inexpensively? My first obvious instinct took us to Marks & Spencer on Oxford Street, where we were told that they usually had them, but, because it was summer, they weren't in the store. (This fact amazed every local we met: "Are they somehow unfamiliar with summer in Britain?!") Another store nearby had very nice boots indeed—for 125 pounds a pair.

Finally, at the suggestion of the shopgirls at M&S, we headed to a store in Marble Arch called Primark. It reminded me of a cross between H&M and Target. Everything was ridiculously cheap and the store was mobbed with tourists, including the Soundgarden fans on their way to Hyde Park who were trying on boots as we arrived in the shoe department. Primark sold exactly one design of Wellington boot for both men and women, emblazoned with British flags. We might as well have worn neon signs reading I AM A TOURIST, and every British fan we met knew exactly where we'd bought them. But we were were now equipped for Hyde Park, no matter how stupid we looked.

* * *

"DO NOT RUN," said the disembodied female voice over the PA, echoing through the long tent that covered the ticket scanners and the security guards at Hard Rock Calling. There were at least 20 different barricaded entry points, and to my eyes, it looked like all of them were going to open up at 12 noon.

Representatives from Live Nation (the promoter) had promised the people who ran the overnight queue that the first three lines, containing the first few hundred fans, would get a three-to-five minute head start. We were in one of those lines, but things did not look particularly promising right now. I overheard security saying there were 2,000 people queued up.

If you go on Google Maps, and click the satellite view of Hyde Park in London, you'll see a photograph of the setup for Hard Rock Calling in 2009. This was the image that I used as a workout goal starting last December. People thought I was kidding when I told them I was doing this, but it made perfect sense to me. It may not have been the New York City Marathon, but being able to get a good spot at Hyde Park was important enough to motivate me through months of sessions at the gym.

As the clock inched towards noon, we moved into tactical position. Glenn moved in front of me, because he likes going on 150 mile bike rides for fun. We divided up the supplies, Glenn taking the lighter bag with the snacks (nuts and crisps and chocolate), and I took the heavier bag with the drinks.

There was movement up at the front and our queue began to move forward. I didn't bother to look to see if any of the other gates were also opening, because it just would have made me more nervous than I already was.

Our queue inched forward at a snail's pace. The ticket scanners weren't working, or were working erratically, or more likely, the nervous security person with the scanner was overwhelmed at six people shoving their tickets at her at the same time.

Glenn got his ticket scanned, moved through security and the bag check, and started running. I got my ticket scanned, got through security and the bag check, and started running. Security guards stood at strategic locations yelling, "DO NOT RUN," while we (and everyone around us) began our quarter-mile sprint across the field to the stage.

jog jog jog. jog jog jog.

I had tested my pace in the ridiculous rubber boots earlier, running in the grass, practicing. I knew I needed to jog lightly, on my toes, at a slower pace than I was used to. This wasn't just because of the boots, but was because of the cubic tons of tree bark on the ground, placed there earlier in the week to absorb the mud.

jog jog jog. jog jog jog.

People in rain ponchos were running fast and passing me, but then I would end up passing them a few seconds later when they stopped to catch their breath, winded. (They were also not very aerodynamic.)

jog jog jog. jog jog jog.

I focused on the most direct route to the stage, which was not a straight line. Other people just ran at full throttle blindly, only to careen into a safety barrier one-third of the way back from the stage, and then have to re-orient themselves. I might have run slower, but I could see where I was going.

jog jog jog. jog jog jog.

I passed the middle security barrier and then I could see the front of the stage. Still jogging forward, I scanned the sides of the stage on Stevie's side, which is where we had planned on standing. I didn't see Glenn, and started to panic he had to go to the other side. I tried to keep calm and focus.

Then I saw him, straddling two spots along the center runway! It was a better spot than I had expected, which was why I couldn't find him at first. I picked up speed and hopped up onto the barrier platform next to him. I looked over the barrier and could not believe we were so close, and could not stop the smile stretching across my face. I was not even that winded.

Glenn was also smiling. "I can't believe it," he said, "You were only 90 seconds behind me!" I couldn't believe it either, because it felt like I was running for hours.

We were in the front row for Hard Rock Calling. I stood there, catching my breath, letting it all soak in, still dumbfounded that our plans actually worked.

We were next to girls from Norway—Hanne and Lisa—who recognized us from Prague, which made us instant friends. (Lisa had a sign in Prague reading, "Bruce, did you meet my mother in 1990?" which he liked quite a bit.) Our alliance quickly became very useful when the rest of the fans were let in. The people who didn't queue early and didn't have numbers were angry that the numbered fans got let in first, and tried to push their way through. There was lots of complaining, and glares at people with numbers on their hands. After a few minutes, everyone calmed down, and made a little room for themselves and everyone else. It was going to be a long day.

The area at the front of the stage filled up very, very quickly, and after the initial rush I decided to make the very long trip to the toilets. "Remember the American accent in the bright pink rain jacket," I said every few feet, trying to smile and make eye contact. "Because I'm coming back this way." There was a woman carrying an umbrella with the Chicago skyline, reading WINDY CITY, at the edge of the crowd. I pleaded with her to keep the umbrella up for the next ten minutes so I could find my way back.

Once I got out past the center crush, I realized that there weren't actually that many people there. There were plenty of people camped out, sitting down on tarps and plastic bags. But in the ten minutes it took me to make the trip to the toilets at the edge of the field and get back to my approximate location, it became a very difficult, careful walk back, with "Excuse me" and

"Hey, it's the American in the pink rain jacket!" every two feet, and lots of nasty looks in response.

(The rain jacket was very, *very* pink. For someone who usually wears the downtown New York City uniform of blacks and grays, it was a little bit bright. But it was on sale, and I didn't realize how pink it was until it arrived. I didn't think it would matter, because I was hopeful I wouldn't be wearing it that much. At least it made me easy to spot in photographs.)

I finally get back to our spot, and look at the plastic bag with the three bottles of water and two bottles of Coke, and wince. It was only 12:30 p.m. but it was very clear that we would not be able to move from our spots for any reason from this point onward. We do not drink one sip of liquid until well Bruce after gets onstage, and even then, do so very, very carefully. We carried most of the drinks we brought in back out with us at the end of the night.

We are planners. We do research. We are skeptics. So, to this day I do not understand how we got such bad information about Hyde Park, specifically how intense the crowd would be. I am grateful to the U.K. fans near us in the queue who set us straight earlier in the day, because otherwise we would have been in trouble. Despite what we had been told by others, there was absolutely no moving from your spot after about 1 p.m. or so. Not to stretch your legs, not to get food, not to pee, not to try to find your friends further back. I was happy to see our advisors on the big screen during the show, in good spots on the rail along one of the sides.

* * *

Hard Rock Calling, Hyde Park, London, 14 July 2012

Support: Lady Antebellum, Tom Morello, John Fogerty

Setlist: Thunder Road (piano), Badlands, We Take Care of Our Own, Wrecking Ball, Death to My Hometown (with Tom Morello), My City of Ruins, Spirit in the Night, The Promised Land (with John Fogerty), Take 'Em As They Come, Jack of All Trades (with Tom Morello), Empty Sky, Because the Night, Johnny 99, Darlington County, Working on the Highway, Shackled and Drawn, Waitin' on a Sunny Day, Raise Your Hand, The River, The Ghost of Tom Joad (with Tom Morello), The Rising (with Tom Morello), Land of Hope and Dreams (with Tom Morello)

Encore: We Are Alive, Born in the U.S.A., Born to Run, Glory Days, Dancing in the Dark, I Saw Her Standing There (with Sir Paul McCartney), Twist and Shout (with Sir Paul McCartney)

Despite the multiple acts and multiple stages, Hard Rock Calling isn't a festival in the strict sense of the word, with ticket sales driven by the headlining act. I was hoping that Bruce felt that way too, and wasn't going to be constructing a festival-type setlist directed at a mixed crowd of fans and casual onlookers. I shouldn't have worried, but I also didn't expect him to stroll onstage holding only a harmonica and talk about how this was the first thing he'd played when his feet first touched down on "English soil," and then Roy hits the chords to "Thunder Road." No band, no guitar, just Bruce and Roy, and it was a tremendous moment. Who else tries this in front of 60,000 people? Where else could Bruce get away with this, besides in Europe? Everyone stood in rapt attention and time genuinely stood still. The sun had come out and the sky was blue and I thought if this was the only notable thing about tonight's gig, I would be happy.

But there would be many other special interludes in the show. John Fogerty came out for "Promised Land," after Bruce had joined him during his opening set earlier in the day for "Rockin' All Over The World" (their first performance of that song together, giving me my big Live Aid moment in London, which was pretty amazing). Tom Morello, also on the bill as support, popped on and off the stage to recreate several of his *Wrecking Ball* contributions, as well as just hanging out and enjoying playing alongside Steve Van Zandt (who also appeared to be having a good time with him).

There were many signs held aloft, but only one sign request, beginning with Bruce asking "Where's the guy with that sign?" (which of course resulted in every sign in the crowd being held up). It was a sign for "Take 'Em As They Come," created by a fan from Spain. ("Where you from, buddy? Spain? Yeah, that figures," Bruce said.) He had the name of the song, along with a list of all of the cities he had brought the sign to, crossing them out and adding the next city. Bruce brought the sign onstage, and began to narrate the list of cities. "Came all the way to Madrid—that's a big investment now, my friend--nope, no song. Paris? No fuckin' good. Got to see the Eiffel Tower though. But London? Tonight, my friend…"

The big screens kept cutting to the fan in the front row along the rail and the disbelief registering on his face; the crowd liked the guy and the story, so that when Bruce explained, "It's completely obscure. I wrote it for *The River*, I thought I needed more rock songs," he had the entire crowd on his side. I am sure someone in the back who didn't recognize the song said, "Let's get a footlong hotdog" (something else Bruce made reference to a few times due to several stands with gigantic signs advertising them). But it is a good song, and a worthwhile request, and was played exceptionally well, down to the flourishes at the end. (It had been soundchecked at least once in the past few weeks.) The band,

Garry and Steve especially, had big smiles on their faces the entire time.

The rail had been set up with a large center walkway area, with a set of steps down from the main stage to another platform extending out. There were also walkways along the rails in the front and all the way out in the center of the crowd. Bruce seemed to find the setup amusing, and made a few jokes about the stairs (references to Indiana Jones and "I didn't know I'd be getting married today.") But he spent a lot of time in all of those locations, especially once it started raining again. He made up a song about how much he liked to play in the rain. He talked about loving the rain. He loved the rain, and he made us forget the rain.

Truthfully, when the raindrops start sluicing down off of your hood onto your face, and your hands start to get waterlogged, you fight hard to ignore it, because it is not a lot of fun. You understand why Bruce works so hard in these rainy shows, making sure that the show is so amazing that you overlook all of that. It occurred to me when I was beaming during "The Ghost of Tom Joad" (with Morello's guest appearance, of course) that it was absolutely pouring rain and that it wasn't bothering me. I sang along during "Sunny Day," the song in the Springsteen catalog I hate the most (probably even more than "The Angel") , the moment in the show I always dread, because it was a stellar version. Nothing lost focus. Nothing went on too long. He didn't have to work the crowd too hard for a vocal response, because he was already receiving one.

Bruce made repeated trips far down along the sides of the stage—not because he had to, but because even out there, the audience was energetic and engaged. Of course, there was also no language barrier tonight, which had to help. But he still worked it hard, out in the crowd, out in the rain, not hiding under the canopy. He brought the horns down front for "Johnny

99." He dragged a reluctant Steve out there during the encore. He carefully escorted Cindy in her high heels down for "Shackled and Drawn." This solidarity with the rest of us getting rained on was repaid, loudly and vocally. Standing in the rain for one or two songs is lip service; making repeated appearances out from under the protection of the stage canopy is just plain admirable (and borderline crazy).

The evolution of "Spirit In The Night" into a regular setlist stalwart instead of an occasional, East Coast-only special treat is wonderful. I love that more people are getting to hear this song. I love that the band are playing it every night again and as a result, it's become stronger and they play it better each time. The interlude with Jake has become a permanent bit. Tonight Bruce enticed him down to the stairs (before it was raining), where Bruce reclined back on them, staring up at the sky. Suddenly, he said, "You know, you're too young—I don't think you were even born, when me and your uncle–" before going into the last verse.

It was heartbreaking. It was real and raw and reminded us all (not that we needed to be reminded) of how big this loss still is for Bruce. He turned the song into yet another tribute to Clarence. (Of course you could argue that the entire tour is a tribute to him, and you would be right.) But he did this in front of Hyde Park, you know? It happened in front of tens of thousands of people, and he never lost the focus of the song. The lengthy intro I had so disliked in Paris has grown on me; it's gotten tighter and more focused. Bruce veers from television preacher to Al Green to Sam Cooke and back again, and relishes every second of it. The backup singers get their chance to shine; it's is a great example of this organism that has grown and coalesced over the course of the tour.

I confess that I was rooting hard for "London Calling," with Tom Morello to be in the encore. Obviously, this had already happened when Bruce opened with that song in 2009. But there is precedent: Morello was onstage with Bruce when he played it at the Rock and Roll Hall of Fame 25th anniversary concerts, and Morello had specifically invoked Joe Strummer during his opening set. That would have been my own perfect, ultimate moment, getting to hear "London Calling" in London. That was about as far as I was going to reach today, and then I heard the words, "I'd like to bring out a special guest—Paul McCartney!"

The entire crowd went berserk, instantly. Everyone had a camera or a phone in the air and everyone tried very very hard to let everyone get their photo. For me, it was this combination of freaking out while being in total disbelief that I was in Hyde Park and here is AN ACTUAL BEATLE, IN LONDON. I wanted to take a million photographs. I wanted to dance like crazy. I wanted to sing and not have to worry about ruining a video. I tried to do all of it, because it was AN ACTUAL BEATLE SINGING BEATLES SONGS IN LONDON. I was at Shea Stadium when Bob Dylan walked out onstage; I love Bob, but Paul's surprise appearance trumped that.

In the end, when the sound went out, I thought there was some problem caused by the center microphone being out on the platform in the rain. Never in a million years did I (or anyone else) think that they would turn the sound off on Bruce Springsteen. But then his monitor engineer made an appearance onstage and made it clear even to us in the crowd that that was what had happened. Even after the line or two of "Goodnight, Irene," I thought that surely the sound would come back on. Everyone was dumbfounded, and it took people a very long time to realize that it was actually over, and that they needed to leave. I wanted to bend down and get a bottle of water after going nine hours without drinking anything, but there was no room to do so. No one could believe it was over like that.

The power being cut impacted the front of the crowd far less than the people in the back, because they started cutting the sound from the relay towers in the field first, and only cut the sound at the stage at the end, by which point the song was finished and Paul McCartney had left the stage. I was annoyed on principle, but far less upset than I would have been had the sound cut out for me in the middle of "Twist and Shout." I felt terrible for the fans for whom this might have been their only show and didn't get to see "Tenth Avenue Freeze-Out" (which was likely the next song) and pay tribute to Clarence.

Lost in all of this, of course, is the fact that this was a fantastic show above and beyond the special guests or the once-in-a-lifetime moments. The essential power of the core set was tremendous. The London set was a perfect example of how to construct a stadium set that will work, and work well, connecting to the diehards in the front hanging on the rail, as well as the casual fans all the way in the back sitting on blankets and eating footlong hotdogs.

I went to sleep thinking: I saw a Beatle singing Beatles songs, onstage in London, with Bruce Springsteen and the E Street Band. I must be doing something right.

* * *

After the show was over and we got back to the hotel, the first thing we did was to stop on the door mat just inside the lobby doors and remove our boots. We promptly dumped them into a garbage bag, and asked the clerk at the front desk if he could please throw it out. It would have been too big for any of the garbage cans in our room, and I did not want that mud in the room under any circumstances.

He was looking at us disapprovingly, when another couple entered the hotel, stopped on the door mat, and removed their mud-covered hiking boots. They picked them up and carried them, traveling towards the elevator in their socks.

That was when another clerk came over and took the bag from us, nodding.

(Hotels did not know quite what to do with us, with our odd comings and goings, our complaints about the internet at 2 a.m., and our utter disinterest in organized tours or dinner reservations or sightseeing advice, or any of the kinds of things a lot of tourists want. In Prague, after watching us go in and out of the hotel about a dozen times in one day, carrying camp chairs over our shoulders, the front desk clerk finally asked us if we needed any assistance—stopping just short of asking us what exactly we were doing, although I'm sure he was dying to.)

We quarantined our clothes, washed our hands in the hottest water we could stand for about 10 minutes straight, and after sending out multiple OMG PAUL MCCARTNEY messages to everyone we could think of, ran out to get food—any kind of food. The chip shop next door seemed like *haute cuisine* given our current state of hunger; given that it was on the main artery to Paddington Station and ridiculously crowded, we grabbed our fish and chips and ate it on the floor of the impossibly tiny hotel room.

We usually always file our show reports before eating, or did both at the same time. After 12 hours of not eating real food, we were pretty sure that it would be understood that we needed to eat first. I do not think I could have strung two words together before getting some food in my stomach.

Once we finished the *Backstreets* reports, needing to spend more time on photos and videos than we usually did, it became another one of those nights we didn't want to end. We stayed up emailing and messaging friends in the States and on the Continent. We went through our photos again and again, until we were too tired to keep our eyes open any longer.

* * *

It was a wonderful, historical night, but Hyde Park was an absolutely miserable place to see a concert. I understood why a lot of fans told me that they were skipping this show, and was grateful we hadn't made the trek previously, either to see Bruce in 2009 or anyone else in other years. Everyone around us rallied remarkably and most people were very prepared with the kind of rain gear you need for wilderness camping; the bright orange emergency survival blanket one person had did not seem excessive once it started to pour.

This year was especially brutal, with the mud, the poor footing, the needing to stand all day because of the mud and the poor footing, the smell of the mud and the bark and the alcohol and other things I would rather not think about. I have never seen a Springsteen gig where so many people were taken out in stretchers. None of this seems necessary, nor can I see how it enhances the experience of the actual concert.

Admittedly, I do not understand the British obsession with the festival. I fail to understand how the musical experience is improved by mud and outdoor toilets. Personally, I would always rather wait to see a band play their own show to their audience, than sit through a festival setlist designed to please the largest common denominator. It makes good business sense and I understand why bands do it, and festivals are incredibly lucrative. It just isn't an experience that is attractive or interesting to me.

* * *

The next morning we both felt like we had been run over by a bulldozer. We had more sightseeing to do, but we also had a week's worth of laundry on our hands, and this was the only day to get both of them done.

"Oh, the glamour," I said, standing in the launderette near the hotel. "Last night, Paul McCartney from the front row. This morning, I fold socks."

The highlight of my Sunday was finally visiting the location of the cover of *Ziggy Stardust and the Spiders from Mars*, something I had been searching for for years. The second highlight of my Sunday was a long nap in the late afternoon, while Glenn went off to see Big Ben and Buckingham Palace and the other mandatory tourist sights.

Over an Indian dinner in a restaurant near the hotel, Glenn and I talked about our plans for Dublin, and were in firm agreement: we were not going to queue. We'd had two great front row experiences, and were utterly wiped out. It would be good to have some down time and enjoy Dublin.

Chapter 6: Dublin

Monday, 16 July 2012

We were standing on the train platform in Dublin, en route to the venue, when Glenn noticed a guy sitting on a bench with a number written on his hand. "What time is the next check-in?" he asked, walking over to him.

The guy first looked surprised, and a little frightened, and then calmed down once he realized how we'd figured out where he was going.

We weren't going to queue in Dublin, and were happy with that decision, until we ran into a horde of American Bruce tourists at Heathrow. We heard them at a distance, talking so loudly you had to notice them. We heard every word of their conversation when we sat down at the gate, talking about where Bruce stays in Dublin, and all about Hyde Park (even though they weren't actually at the show), and all about their arduous journey from the East Coast to London.

It was one of those times that I wanted to go hide or apologize to everyone that not all of us were actually like that. I realized that given the proximity to the East Coast, the time of year, the fact that were two shows and the ease of travel (you didn't have to worry about a language barrier) made the Dublin shows an attractive destination for U.S. fans. I realize they were excited, but it came across as overbearing; there were plenty of

Wrecking Ball shirts sitting at the gate who weren't audibly broadcasting their presence, and by extension, their authority. We came to Europe to see shows with Europeans, not to transplant Secaucus or South Philly to the other side of the ocean.

* * *

We had absolutely underestimated what Hyde Park was going to take out of us physically, that it would be different than queuing for a regular show, that we would be on our feet for ten hours straight. We were still doing all right when we arrived in Dublin and headed out to the venue to check in. If our numbers had been too high, our decision would have been an easy one. But they were just good enough to potentially get a rail spot between the side platforms or be two deep in the center, and we couldn't say no.

Once again, we were still determined to get some sightseeing done between check-ins. I had visited Dublin in the '80s, so luckily I had already seen most of the tourist obligations. We had to cut our list down to anything we could see near the hotel and various U2-related sites (like the Bonavox Hearing Aid shop, the place that Bono guy got his name from, and an exhibit of rare, early U2 photographs). We gave up on anything historical or literary, skipped the Phil Lynott statue, and passed on visiting a pub that writer friends in the States had recommended. We saw some of Temple Bar, and we had afternoon tea, but we definitely did not get enough of a sense of what Dublin was like in 2012. We were just too tired.

I was grateful that being so far north it stayed light until late, giving us bonus sightseeing time after the 8 p.m. check-in; I was equally grateful to see our old friend Tesco across the street from the hotel, making it easy to provision for the queue.

* * *

On our way back to the train station after the 8 p.m. check-in, we passed The Four Seasons and another hotel, just steps from the venue. I stared longingly at both of them, and envied the five-minute walk the fans staying at those places would have. By the time we got back to the hotel, I was shivering and feverish. Glenn said we should give up our spots. I said I would nap and we would see how I felt after the midnight check-in.

He relented. "You didn't hesitate, so you must not feel too bad."

I did, actually, feel that bad, but adrenaline and determination were still on my side.

When the alarm went off the next morning at 6:30 a.m., I still felt terrible, but wasn't ready to give up on the queue. I thought there would be time to get some sleep in between check-ins. There was one at 8 a.m., and if all went well, there would be one at noon; after that, we would be there for the duration. Instead, we had to be back at 11 a.m., giving me just enough time to shower and eat breakfast. After that check-in, they told us to leave, but be back by 1:30 p.m. That was not enough time to go back to the hotel. I just wanted to fall down on the grass nearby and sleep.

That's when Glenn said, "We're having lunch at the Four Seasons."

I like to think that I can walk into most places with enough self-esteem to seem like I belong there, but that didn't account for dragging my tired self wearing a fleece pullover and a bright pink rain jacket into a five-star hotel. You would think that the Four Seasons would look askance at our street rat selves, with our uneven tans and layers of clothing (it was the coldest it had been the entire trip earlier that morning), but they didn't seem to care. We felt a little bit out of place for about five minutes, until other people wearing *Wrecking Ball* or other tour t-shirts started filtering in and sitting down themselves. I started to relax and feel human again.

We sat there until almost 1 p.m., then got back into the barricades for the check-in. The fact that I'd had a comfortable chair to sit in for almost two hours, not to mention hot tea and delicious sandwiches, did me a world of good. I felt recharged.

But I still fell asleep on the pavement at some point after the 1:30 p.m. check-in, and slept for at least 45 minutes as the rest of the queue revolved around me. When I say "sleep," I mean that I was sound asleep. Bruce could have showed up to say hello to the queue and I am serious when I tell you that I would have taken the opportunity to get more sleep. It was exactly what I needed to give me just a little bit more energy, but I still almost killed a friend from the tour when he came up later asking where he would see us next. "Really," we kept saying, "We have to go home!"

We met amazing people in the queue, including a grey-haired gentleman from Cork with the most beautiful Irish lilt. He crossed himself while telling me about his visit to the World Trade Center the one time he visited New York City. He was a big fan of bluegrass and country music, loved Neil Young and Bob Dylan, and treated us like we were neighbors. We successfully avoided talking to the group of American fans near us who kept lecturing the Europeans about how much nicer the fans were in the States.

When we're not running around following Bruce Springsteen, we like to travel around the States seeing the different baseball parks. When we do this, we are almost always wearing something that advertises that we are fans of the baseball team from New York (and no, not the Yankees). As a result, every time we visit a ballpark outside of the Eastern Seaboard, without fail, someone wants to talk to me about 9/11. They don't want to have a discussion or hear how a New Yorker feels about it, they just want to be able to say their piece to someone actually from New York and be done with it. I just let them talk and wait for it to be over, and pray for something to happen in the game that will give me an excuse not to respond.

No one in Europe ever wanted to talk to me about 9/11. They wanted to talk about their trip or trips to New York City (it seems like every Springsteen fan I met had been to the 2009 Giants Stadium shows) and how much they loved it. In the States, people not from New York always ask something like "Do you like it there?" and when my answer is that I love it or that I wouldn't live anywhere else, they seem surprised. In Europe—in Dublin especially—there is a knowing nod and zero umbrage when I call it the greatest city in the world, and they never ask if I like living there. Of course, in Dublin, literally every person we met had a cousin or a sister or an uncle who was in New York or Chicago or somewhere else (always somewhere remote like Tulsa).

Dublin was the first place where I felt that the fans held a real, deep love for Bruce Springsteen and his music. I realize that Bruce's Irish heritage helps, but even eavesdropping on casual fans chatting on their phones on the train after the show, I heard people talking about how much they liked the new songs or how happy they were to hear "The Rising." The woman working at the check-in counter at the airport lit up when we mentioned we had been in Ireland to see Bruce, upgraded our seats, and told us how upset she was that she didn't get to hear her favorite song, which was "If I Should Fall Behind," not "Glory Days" or "Dancing In The Dark."

* * *

From my perspective, the Dublin queue was great, with the involvement of the venue security early on. It was such a marked contrast to how fans in the U.S. are treated by venue security at concerts. Sure, there were some idiots working in security, just like there are idiots working in every field everywhere, but have you ever waited in a line to get into a concert and had a security guard present you with a box of cookies to go with your tea? Because that's the kind of thing that happened in Dublin. It wasn't perfect, and I later heard tales of chicanery and corruption at the front of the line. But for most people, it was a respectful, humane queue.

The Dublin crowd around us the first night would probably have been fine if Bruce had not come out to greet the crowd on the side of the stage when he arrived. This meant that everyone who had been sitting calmly on the ground rushed forward and sideways and those who didn't used that opportunity to improve their standing position. We suddenly had people with numbers higher than 700 standing right behind behind us, whose numbers were in the 160's. We had people with no numbers and children in tow (who would later take flasks out of backpacks) right behind us. There was no sense of solidarity and having toughed it out through check-ins with these people; they just knew we had a better spot than they did, and they wanted to try to get it. It got weird and ugly at times like no other show had this tour, with a parade of drunk people trying to shove their way through. Security was not helpful at all, or was only reluctantly helpful. It was an unwelcome detraction from a strong and enjoyable show.

* * *

RDS Arena, Dublin, Ireland, 17 July 2012

Setlist: Twist and Shout (cont. from London), I Fought the Law, Badlands, Out in the Street, We Take Care of Our Own, Wrecking Ball, Death to My Hometown, My City of Ruins, Spirit in the Night, I'm a Rocker, Prove It All Night, Darkness on the Edge of Town, Jack of All Trades, Murder Incorporated, Johnny 99, Easy Money, Working on the Highway, Waitin' on a Sunny Day, Raise Your Hand, My Hometown, The River, The Rising, Land of Hope and Dreams

Encore: We Are Alive, Born in the U.S.A., Born to Run, Rosalita (Come Out Tonight), Dancing in the Dark, Tenth Avenue Freeze-out, Twist and Shout, American Land

The band was in excellent form and high spirits tonight, coming out in sunglasses against the glare of the still-bright sunlight. Patti was back, making fans around us happy they would get to see "Easy Money."

While waiting for the show to begin, we saw something unfamiliar being wheeled out and placed near the front of the drum riser. From my position I could just make out the top of it, and the word "ON". Once the band were onstage, Steve and Bruce went back to the drum riser and moved the mystery item to the front of the stage. That's when we saw that it was a giant electrical switch, with the switch flipped to the OFF position. The crowd immediately understood, breaking out in cheers and laughter. With exaggerated movements and accompanying ridiculous facial gestures, Bruce and Steve brought the switch to the "ON" position, and Bruce stepped to the microphone.

"Before we were so rudely interrupted," he said, as the band picked up at the second to last verse of "Twist and Shout," and the audience exploded with excitement and energy, as though they had been waiting for this very occasion. In some ways, they had; whether or not you had been at the show in London, the umbrage was universal. There were at least 20 different signs in the crowd making reference to curfews or plugs being pulled, with my favorite being simply "FECK THE CURFEW." Aside from Steve Van Zandt's cascade of Tweets trying to explain, and then explain again, and then explain one more time, there had been no official response from the Springsteen camp for three days.

Until now.

Once "Twist and Shout" finished, Bruce got in one more dig before getting down to business, launching into "I Fought The Law." (It was the first time it had been played this tour and the first time I had ever seen E Street play it.) The joke was not lost on anyone, and Bruce was making us all part of the punchline tonight. "Let that be a lesson to 'em!" he shouted at the song's conclusion.

The rest of the set was absolutely solid and on track: choice pairings of "Prove It All Night" into "Darkness On The Edge of Town" and "Murder Incorporated" into "Johnny 99," sign requests for "I'm A Rocker" and "My Hometown," both making their tour premieres. The guitar battle during "Murder" was insane, Nils and Bruce battling each other to an incendiary finish. "My Hometown" was dedicated to "my favorite Irishmen," and before I had a heart attack (really, it would have just been too much) Bruce informed us that U2 weren't in the country. "The River" continues to be an astounding moment in Europe. It echoes, it howls, the crowd sings this one with feeling each and every time.

The entire encore is a powerhouse, a steamrolling hit parade. "Born In The USA" is the one song guaranteed to get people out of their chairs in the stands, and you remember just how enormous that album was at a time when we had only just coined the term "global jukebox." "Rosalita,"another request, fit perfectly into the jubilant atmosphere and was a nice change of pace. "Dancing In The Dark" is too good to hate, and for the first time ever, I knew the person invited onstage to dance with Bruce; it wasn't a kid being pimped out by their parents or a girl brought off her boyfriend's shoulders, but a gray-haired fan in her 60's who had been following the European tour.

During the encore, the video screens on the side switched to closeups of the "electrical switch," showing the switch flipped to ON. We thought it was just yet another continuation of the joke from earlier, except that two people dressed as a London police officer and another as a London city official came onstage and brandished paperwork at Bruce and Steve, trying to prevent them from playing "Twist and Shout." They are waved off the stage, with much theatrical ripping of the paperwork. One of the many signs referring to the curfew, reading ONLY THE BOSS SAYS WHEN TO PULL THE PLUG, is brought onto the stage. The encore continued without incident until after "Tenth Avenue Freeze-out," when the "London officials" returned, and staged a mock battle between themselves and Bruce and Steve. The switch went off; the switch went on; the switch went off, and all four mock-wrestle to the ground, before a young boy comes on the stage and flips the switch back to the "ON" position, and the band goes into "American Land" to finish the set.

The E Street Band is playing so well. Every performance is rock solid. The only misses tonight were a few vocal flubs (that and the constant nose blowing makes me wonder if he has a cold; Bruce's voice sounded okay, but perhaps just the tiniest bit tired). It was a thoroughly solid and enjoyable outing, with the business of needing to make a statement about Hyde Park—and continuing to make that statement at the beginning and end of the show—taking precedence, and everything has a cost. To be fair, the controversy needed to be addressed: the fans expected it to be addressed, and this was the best possible way to address it, instead of press representatives and statements to the media. But now that it is out of the way, the decks are cleared for a brilliant second night show tomorrow.

* * *

RDS Arena, Dublin, Ireland, 18 July 2012

Setlist: This Hard Land (solo acoustic), No Surrender, Two Hearts, The Ties That Bind, We Take Care of Our Own, Badlands, Something in the Night, Adam Raised a Cain, Wrecking Ball, Death to My

Hometown, My City of Ruins, Spirit in the Night, Jackson Cage, She's the One, Jack of All Trades, Atlantic City, Because the Night, Darlington County, Easy Money, Waitin' on a Sunny Day, The Promise (solo piano), The River, Backstreets, Land of Hope and Dreams

Encore: Born in the U.S.A., Born to Run, Glory Days, Seven Nights to Rock, Dancing in the Dark, Tenth Avenue Freeze-out, Rocky Ground, American Land

The rain had stopped and the skies had cleared and we heard the guitar before we saw Bruce coming out onstage, strumming "This Hard Land," solo acoustic in the sunlight for Dublin. "This Hard Land," and suddenly no opening song could possibly be any better for any place, and we knew this one was going to be a keeper.

Just in case we weren't sure, he led with a powerhouse combination to reel in the crowd: "No Surrender," "Two Hearts" (with extra oomph from Stevie), and "The Ties That Bind," so that when he went into "We Take Care Of Our Own," the entire audience was fully engaged. Next came "Badlands," sealing the deal.

When"Something In The Night" followed, you wouldn't be alone in thinking of the setlist the second night in Paris. It wasn't Paris—it was outside, it was twice as big, and it was still light out—but it was everything the first night in Dublin wasn't (and night one was still a fine, fine show). Night one was, however, overwhelmed by the distraction of Hyde Park and the need to make a statement without making a statement, and I think it got in the way just a little. The crowd clearly loved the business with the switch (and the fans near us tonight told us they hoped he did it again so they could see it) but there was definitely an impact on the show.

Bruce hits a familiar chord; I know what it is but am surprised. It was "Adam Raised A Cain," and you would think this wouldn't work in a stadium while it was still light out, but it does, there was sufficient intensity and darkness, with a blistering solo that had Bruce pounding the body of the guitar in satisfaction when it was done. You were ready for a cigarette by the time Bruce decided to bring out "Wrecking Ball," "Death to my Hometown," and "My City of Ruins." It was during the roll call in the latter that something clicked and I realized that the Apollo Medley had been AWOL since Paris. This then led me to thinking about how sad I was that Michele Moore didn't get more to do onstage. (This would be very funny to recall later.)

Tonight we did not queue. Instead, we arrived just after the queues had been let in and found a likely spot about even with Patti's mic, about 20 rows back. The key was that the people in front of us were short. Things were fine, until we started chatting with the women in front of us (who had travelled down from near Belfast) and they informed us that the two tall people in front of them had their daughters in tow, and had told everyone around them that the girls would be on their shoulders for the entire night. The ladies soon moved right in front of the parents, but then we had to maneuver ourselves away from them. Eventually, I went to one side, where we were now between the parents and a bunch of 20-something dudes who had smuggled in at least four bottles of vodka.

I chose to just make friends with the drunk guys, and it was the best decision we could have made. They were fans; they had been to the shows in 2009, they had dragged their non-fan friend with (who wanted to talk with us about Jay-Z and Kanye instead). They weren't bad guys, they were just 20-something dudes who wanted to party at the Springsteen show. They became our staunchest allies against the parents, who were shortly defeated soundly by the three 20-something girls behind them who wanted to jump up and down and sing every single song the entire night. The parents finally gave up and dropped back, and the girls moved up right behind us. (The plan of holding the daughters on their shoulders all night lasted for less than half a song.)

The ringleader of the 20-something girls kept apologizing for bumping into us and we kept telling her that it wasn't a problem, and that they were great. Every time Bruce's ass was on the big screen, they would all shout that he needed to come back here and show it to them up close. Everyone around us would encourage them and offer their own commentary on Bruce's ass and the desirability of him bringing the ass back into the crowd for the girls. But the girls knew every word to every song, and never stopped smiling. We would smile at each other and we would sing together and we would jump up and down together like we had been best Bruce friends forever. I loved them.

"Spirit" was wavering a little, it was not the most focused introduction, but it was a fine "Spirit In The Night" nonetheless. Due to Jake's unfortunate incident (Bruce informed us that he sneezed during the encore the previous night and had a back spasm) he was wheeled out onto the stage and was confined to a stool on the horn riser for the night) he couldn't join Bruce for an exploration down at the front. Instead, Bruce sang to him from there:
"Jake, are you back there?"
horn melody
"How's the back?"
blerp
Bruce cracked up, and went back to join him in solidarity.

A sign commemorating a fan's 100th show resulted in "Jackson Cage," which Bruce had to have been thinking about in advance in a segment that included "Jackson Cage," "She's The One," "Jack of All Trades," and "Atlantic City." When the drumbeat started for the latter, Glenn turned to the drunk guys and said,

"Hey, who wanted to hear this one?"
"What is it?"
"It's 'Atlantic City'!"
A great HOORAY went up and the culprit came forward and put his arms around two of his friends. His face lit up so brightly it made you just a little misty. And we sang about the Chicken Man together, two kids from Brooklyn and a bunch of kids from Dublin, and it was amazing. It is a great story, no matter where in the world you might be from.

Everyone loves "Because The Night," I'm convinced, and it worked, it worked even going into "Darlington County," which we sang with feeling along with everyone else, cheering every mention of New York City as loudly as the Irish cheered every mention of Dublin. "Sunny Day" had the camerawoman following Bruce around, and Bruce turning and mugging directly into the camera, to which my reaction was, "A Mr. Hewson for you on line three. He says to stop stealing his bit."

The band were set up for something when Bruce changed direction and everyone left and he headed for the piano, and with the initial exploratory chords I realized we were getting Sign Delay Syndrome. I hoped that our Dutch friend who had the sign for this song the night before was still in the audience somewhere, as the sign for "The Promise" came to fruition. That was the one time I wished that the drunk guys were just a little quieter (but they did try to talk quietly, at least) and I'm not sure everyone knew the song (okay, I am actually pretty sure about this) but that instance of Bruce trusting the audience was amazing, and they equally trusted him and gave him the space to play something they might not have known.

The initial chords of "The River" resulted in the loudest crowd roar yet, and great jubilation in our group, from both young and old. The drunk guys pounded each other on the back, yelling, "This is the best song in the world!" Glenn got corralled into their group during the singalong part, arms around him on both sides like he was one of the fellows, which is the best compliment they could have given us (well, besides continually offering us vodka mixed with various things).

"Backstreets!" No, seriously, "Backstreets." Arms in the air, random people jumping up and down in excitement, the spotlight on Bruce, guitar aloft in salute, even if people didn't recognize the song they knew it was an important moment. Everyone shut up. Everyone paid attention. The dancing girls swayed quietly, the drunk guys stood still and did not take their eyes off of the stage.

When the next song was "Land of Hopes and Dreams," my first thought was "Wait, we're at the end of the show?" My second thought was, "Wow, how about that "Promise" / "River" / "Backstreets" segue!" But there were a lot of those tonight, those deliberate sequences and placings, it was a night where Bruce was firing on all cylinders, but excelling most of all in terms of craft, tension, pacing and tone.

"Born In The USA" had everyone going nuts all around us, jumping and dancing and yelling and screaming. I thought, "David Brooks is an asshole." I thought, "David Brooks never stood with a bunch of kids from Dublin singing Bruce Springsteen songs." I thought, "I think David Brooks is actually the one who doesn't understand 'Born In The USA'." Then I stopped thinking and started jumping up and down with the girls. "Born To Run," and the stadium lights come to life and we are all singing together, everyone around us, every single word of every single line. I do not know how anyone anywhere could ever get tired of "Born To Run."

"Glory Days" was exactly what the crowd wanted next, and then it was time for "7 Nights To Rock." No one really knows "7 Nights," but as I have posited in the past, what makes it a good encore number is that it's not tired or worn out and it's easy to pick up on the chorus, which is what everyone around us did, leaving us to sing the lines about the Lion's Den and the Chatterbox. Then we all danced together for "Dancing In The Dark," jumping up and down one more time.

And then, Michele Moore is off the riser and standing next to Bruce and I think that there is no way on God's green earth that they could be planning to perform "Rocky Ground" right now, in front of a stadium, but Max starts hitting the rim of the snare with the drumstick and Bruce starts talking and I wonder how this is going to work and if everyone is going to start talking or leaving or somehow break the magic.

But the magic holds hard, and Michele starts singing and then people quietly join in, singing the chorus, nodding their head, cheering in recognition. The fans know the new songs almost better than the old rarities, they know *Born In The USA* most of all but they know the new record too, and they are happy to hear the new record, because they have also heard just about everything else they had wanted to hear. "Rocky Ground" is still beautiful and powerful and one of my favorite songs since *Tunnel of Love*, and the addition of the horn arrangement, delicate and expansive, remains one of my favorite elements of this show.

We consider starting to make our way towards the exit during "American Land" but everyone around us is having too much fun, and it seems rude. So we stand and clap along politely. Maybe there will be "Twist and Shout," maybe there will be something else (it is time for something else, I think) but "American Land" is it, and the band are leaving. We wait patiently for Jake to be helped off the riser and into the wheelchair and wheeled down the ramp, and once that is done, Bruce waves goodbye. But we are still not rushing towards the exit to get a jump on the crowd, because we are shaking hands with the ladies from Belfast and bro-hugging and shaking hands with the drunk guys, and the dancing girls are hugging us and telling us that they hope to see us in America some day.

It was a fine, fine way to end the European run.

* * *

After Wednesday's show, we were determined to have a decent meal to celebrate our last night of the trip. But every late-night restaurant we knew about was already closed, no longer in business, or simply too far to walk to only to find out it was closed or no longer in business. We headed back to Temple Bar and a hamburger shop we had passed previously.

There was a huge crowd (which, given the lack of late-night food options, didn't surprise me), so there was going to be a considerable wait. It was small and crowded, so I went outside to lean against a wall. Temple Bar is almost the equivalent to Bourbon Street in New Orleans in terms of public drunkenness and loud music being played every few feet. It was fun to stand outside on the corner and observe the idiocy, and listen to the bad singalong at the pub across the street.

A few minutes later, I heard a familiar melody. It took me two seconds to place it before waving at Glenn to come outside.

Glenn walked outside, listened, and his face lit up. "Ha! This is great!"

It was "I Still Haven't Found What I'm Looking For," and was going to be the closest to a U2 experience in Dublin that we were going to have.

He started laughing, hard. I was already laughing.

Our food was finally ready, our last night of eating garbage after a show because we got out too late to get anything better. We grabbed it and walked up the street back to the hotel, singing along to the U2 song loudly and without shame.

Just then, we ran into a group of Bruce fans, the diehards from the front of the queue. We thanked the woman who ran the queue for her hard work, and then saw our friend who had danced with Bruce that night.

"So, are you going to Oslo?" she asked. "I'm thinking about it."

Chapter 7: The Fans

The first night in Paris, I was ready to buy into the myth of the European fan being better in all ways than the U.S. fan: they were overwhelmingly quieter, more participatory, more respectful. There were no mass exoduses during "Jack of All Trades." The only people who talked through the slow or quiet songs were the five people who walked up behind us about ten minutes before the show started and made sure the entire world around them knew they were from Philadelphia.

So, it was easy for me to embrace the established party line hook, line and sinker. I was enchanted… for at least the next 24 hours.

Night two, however, it wasn't chat in East-Coast-accented English I had to *shhhhhhhhhh* during "Something In The Night," it was French and Norwegian. This would prove to not be an anomaly as the tour went on (and there are enough YouTube videos to back me up on this point). European fans were not perfect, and had their own list of annoyances and sins against other fans: Dutch fans blatantly cut in front of me, Italian fans held places for their friends with numbers 800 and higher, a British woman with a fox puppet photobombed every person behind her, trying to get the band's attention, Spanish and Austrian fans would defend their show's status as The Greatest Show Ever fervently and without basis in fact. By the end of the tour, every nationality was guilty of some kind of crime against other fans, being it cheating or talking or pushing or holding signs in someone's face for an entire show.

By the end of my trip I had reached the conclusion that what makes the European experience unique is a combination of diverse elements in the audience as a whole, which creates a different dynamic in Europe.

The fans are younger. There is a large contingent of fans who are ten to twenty years younger than any U.S. audience. There were tour diehards whose first shows were in 2009, or who hadn't turned 21 yet. It is still not the majority of the crowd, but it is getting close to being 50% of it. Someone who hasn't seen "Born To Run" 50 times already is going to have a fresh response to it.

The audience responds more vocally and energetically. The fact of the matter is that there is simply going to be more energy from a crowd when you are dealing with people in their 20s and 30s. But there is also a more participatory tradition at live events like concerts, which many believe has its origins in European football crowds and the kinds of group chanting that goes on there. A stadium or an arena is a place where being loud and boisterous is accepted and encouraged. (This also results in the infernal constant clapping whether a song benefits from audience participation or not, which is not a positive.)

Bruce and the band obviously love the energy from a crowd that is excited and engaged. I have sat behind the stage at enough shows in the States to know how dead the audience can be, even down in the front. In Europe, it was an incredible feeling to be in a crowd who was loud and excited and having fun.

The audience is more diverse. There are more women in the audience in Europe, and there are more women down at the front of the stage in Europe. The majority of the fanbase is still male, but there is a greater diversity across age and sex than in the States. There were people in the crowd from their teens to their 60s, and a wider mix across those ages. In the U.S. you have a small amount of younger fans and small amount of older fans, with the majority in the 40 - 60 age range. Diversity means that the audience reaction will be different throughout the crowd, and that the energy will vary as well. The different responses create an atmosphere that feels lighter and more open.

They consider Springsteen to be a contemporary artist. Bruce is given the respect of an active working artist and is not considered to be to be a legacy act, coasting on songs written 30 years ago. Nor do most younger fans consider it their parents' music (although some do discover it in that manner), but a the music of current, working artist. Fans are not just coming to the shows to just to hear the hits or the songs they grew up with; they expect to hear the new songs and are disappointed when they do not.

There were always cheers of recognition for new material, and I had multiple conversations with fans who were genuinely disappointed that Bruce made a tradeoff between "Easy Money" or "Shackled and Drawn" from the new record, because they wanted to be able to see both of them performed. Compare that attitude to a not-minority opinion among U.S. fans who regard the performances of songs from the new album as a punishment they have to sit through in order to see the older material.

Blues-based traditional rock and roll is not dead. Springsteen fans in Europe are not just Springsteen fans, they are fans of rock and roll and actively listen to music from all eras. I met fan after fan in all of the age groups who agonized over juggling Springsteen gigs (and available cash to buy tickets) with other bands. I saw kids with Clash tattoos and Gaslight Anthem tattoos mixed in with their Springsteen tattoos. Rock is not dead or sleeping over there in any generation. (This is not meant as some rockist assertion of the supremacy of classic rock in the canon, just an observation.)

There is a different relationship with the fans because he isn't one of them. The European fans do not claim ownership of Springsteen in the same way the U.S. audience does. They do not seem to need him to be what he was in 1978 or what he was in 1984 (although the latter is the era most emulated by fans coming to the show, simply because it is one of the most iconic rock and roll images ever). No one lectures another fan along the lines of, "Well, you didn't see him in 1975, you're not a *real fan*," because almost no one saw him in 1975.

They don't take Springsteen for granted. There is an attitude of respect and gratitude that projects through everything: through participation, through listening and not talking, through paying attention, through the days people spend in the queue, through the dedication and investment of time in travel and waiting. These are real, tangible elements that show an artist you respect them that can't be replaced by holding up THANK YOU signs during a show (although they do that too, but usually at the individual level). Not every person in every crowd necessarily knew every song, but their reaction to something new, unfamiliar or quiet was to listen, not to start having a loud conversation with the person next to them. (Even the smokers in Vienna didn't talk.)

In non-English speaking countries, being a fan is hard work. It is one thing to study English in school as a second language, and it is another to speak it and understand it, and it is far beyond that to be able to comprehend art and literature in that second language with fluency. Many fans I spoke with expressed an opinion that they found Bruce's lyrics to be easy to understand, but it still requires spending a lot of time in a language that is not your native tongue. It's hard work, and requires a tangible investment of time and energy.

The fans have more at stake. When you have four shows in your country (one of which is a festival, held on an island), you don't have much choice if you wake up on the day of the concert and it's pouring rain and freezing. The European fans will endure just about anything. They don't leave and they still queue early. Bruce notices and doesn't take it for granted (the "You are fucking die-hards!" comment in Florence, another show performed through torrential rain) and he will, in return, meet them in kind via the performance.

It's easy for me to skip shows at the Meadowlands because I don't like the crowds; I can go to Boston or Philadelphia or Washington, D.C. without very much effort at all. Someone who lives in the North of England either sees the show closest to them or faces not seeing Springsteen at all that tour. Every show matters.

All of these factors, taken in combination with the fact that Springsteen can sell out stadiums almost everywhere he goes in Europe, creates a very special relationship. It's not that the fans are necessarily better, but that the audience as a whole is different in crucial ways that have a direct impact on Bruce and the band's performances in Europe.

* * *

I had hoped to be able to have more opportunities to talk with European fans and dig into my theories, but people were too tired from queuing and didn't want to have intense conversations, and the language barrier made it tough to chat casually with other fans. Your average die-hard European Springsteen fan will have above-average command of the English language just as a matter of survival, but there were also many fans who seemed to have a good command of the written word but were less comfortable speaking. For example, I very much wanted to talk to the large contingent from Poland who showed up at the show in Prague, but only a few of them felt comfortable chatting at length in English, and my Polish is non-existent.

English remained the *lingua franca* in the Springsteen queue, but there was always someone who spoke the language of whoever has just showed up and needed the check-in procedure explained to them. You got used to hearing "Polski!" or "Italia!" and someone getting up and walking over to translate.

* * *

It was very warm in Prague, surprisingly warm. It had rained once earlier in the day, but the rain had not reappeared, and now we were all sitting on the terraplas in front of the stage in the bright sunlight, praying for a cloud. Someone went on a water run, coming back carrying five or six bottles of water. This is not a small feat when—like in the States—the caps have all been removed.

He handed out the bottles of water, and I immediately went into my purse and extracted a handful of bottlecaps; this is what we do in the States, of course, because otherwise your water will fall over and spill and then you either have no water or you have to go buy another bottle. We have a stable of bottle caps in desk drawers and handbags and pockets, and didn't realize until Paris that we would need to acquire the European variant for our run here. It also never occurred to us that this was an international phenomenon.

Sarah, a fan from Wales (by way of the Netherlands), immediately burst out laughing as soon as she saw the bottle caps.

"Now I *know* you're a real Springsteen fan," she said. "Not because of how many shows you have seen or what your favorite album is...but because you have a dozen bottle caps in your purse."

* * *

Springsteen sells a lot of merchandise in Europe. It seemed like every other person had a Bruce shirt of some official vintage; shirts from earlier this tour, shirts from previous tours, shirts from shows in the States. They wore shirts when they signed up for the queue, they wore another shirt in the queue, they wore a shirt to the show. There were homemade shirts, and shirts made by individual country fan alliances: Blood Brothers in Poland, No Surrender in Greece, This Hard Land in Finland. The percentage of shirt-wearers to non-shirt wearers was strikingly high compared to the States, and some people seemed a little bemused that I would wear a shirt by another artist to the show.

There were always plenty of American flags in the crowd, carried by people who seemed to mean well, or were at least enthusiastic about it. (My inner Girl Scout shuddered at the lack of flag etiquette.) Americans didn't bring American flags to shows; they brought signs announcing that they were from Boston or Philadelphia. Europeans would bring the flags of their respective countries, I spotted Greece and Croatia and Italy and Spain and Hungary; I even saw South Africa on the rail at Hyde Park.

I liked playing "name the flag" before the show started each night, picking out fans in the crowd. I didn't like the signs from the American fans. All I could think was, "He plays your city multiple times every single tour, and you want special recognition for traveling? Go talk to the fans from Hungary or Croatia."

The stage structure itself always had two flags, the U.S. flag and the flag of the country, one on each side of the stage. Fans absolutely noticed it, and the local fans always noticed and appreciated the acknowledgment. It was a small effort that meant a lot.

* * *

Every fan, no matter where they are from, has their queue and show survival strategies: some people stop eating or drinking at noon the day of the concert. Others have brought over a suitcase full of 5-hour Energy shots. There is talk about the benefits of effervescent Vitamin C, a discussion about the local equivalent of Gatorade, and analysis how much Ibuprofen you need to get through the show. People had impossibly tiny camp stools or chairs that folded into canes. I do not eat candy and try to stay away from processed sugar, but after a week on the road, the suggestion of having a package of Life Savers to give you an energy boost suddenly seemed genius. The pack of fruit-flavored Mentos in my pocket was a godsend 90 minutes into the show, when the adrenaline boost started to fade.

Being on the road following a band around is a thoroughly un-normal way to live. I have done it for brief periods of time, a handful of shows, but I do not flourish there. It becomes another country. There is another language, there is shorthand, there is code, there are customs and a pecking order. It seems like a world of fun and adventure but I get claustrophobic after a few shows, needing the context of the outside world, not wanting to shut myself off from mundanity.

Most fans following Bruce around Europe focused exclusively on the shows and stayed near the venues, and saw the city as an afterthought (if at all). Other fans who wanted to see the sights did so after the show or bought seats, eliminating the need to queue. We seemed to be the only crazy idiots who tried to combine both queuing for GA and sightseeing. We just didn't want to spend all that money and travel that distance and not see the places we were traveling through. However, I would not recommend this plan to anyone else. We had originally aimed for a 40/60 split between Springsteen and sightseeing, and failed miserably. Seven shows over three weeks seemed like a reasonable pace, but turned out to be far from it.

It may have been smarter to stay near the venue and commute to the sights (instead of vice versa), but I know that if we had done that, we never would have seen anything. You get nervous about leaving the queue; you get tired and unmotivated and don't want to expend the effort to go anywhere. This is not a judgment of anyone who did that; in a lot of ways I wish my personality would be more suited to it. I know what will make me happy and what will make me miserable. The tradeoff is a higher number in the queue, and the subsequent distance from the stage.

It's an addiction; once you've been in the very front row one time, you understand why people do what they do. It is exciting and your heart will pound faster every time Bruce walks to the front of the stage. From a practical standpoint, it's more comfortable, believe it or not; you tend to have more room, you can see everything, there are no signs in your way, you can breathe.

It is great fun in small doses, and I am happy to have done it in Prague and in London, gathering memories for a lifetime, but I could not do it show after show. Given my small window into that world, I completely understand why Bruce took the time to thank the fans in the front in Helsinki, coming out just after the gates were opened to play a special acoustic set and spend quite a lot of time just chatting with and acknowledging the people he genuinely recognized and remembered. (You can find the videos on YouTube.) On the other hand, for many fans, getting to one show can be a significant achievement. But the repeat patronage is definitely, visibly appreciated and acknowledged by Springsteen and other band members. And for a fan, being recognized publicly by your idol is quite understandably seductive.

* * *

We met amazing people. There were fans we met briefly and others we saw throughout our entire trip. There was the father and son who drove over from London for the second night in Paris; hearing our accents, he proceeds to tell a story about being in the States in 1980 and being at the show the night John Lennon died. We met amazing people from Long Island in the queue in Prague, when our New York accents gave us away as we protested the 5 a.m. roll call. We met Dutch fans via Twitter who kindly gave us a ride back to our hotel after the show in the Czech Republic, driving with as much aplomb in the after-show traffic as someone from Brooklyn fighting the traffic on the Belt Parkway. I have exponentially more good stories than negative ones.

Mostly, people were great; mostly, I find that people are great. They shared food , sunscreen, plastic bags, water, taxi rides and countless other things. This is also not that different than the States, where—while there are plenty of fans who only care what you can do to improve their standing spot— there are also people who would go out of their way to get you a copy of a show you needed, or sell you their extra ticket at face value.

Music fans are pretty much exactly the same everywhere in the world.

* * *

It was always fascinating which songs resonated the strongest. The huge response to "Born In The U.S.A." would only seem curious if you were not alive when that record came out and was everywhere, all the time, the biggest thing ever, or if you somehow forgot about the utter world domination of Bruce Springsteen in the '80s. But it also about something so enormous from the other side of the world being here right now, connecting them to something larger than themselves. It is about being proud of where you are from, no matter what problems there might be, it is about striving for meaning behind the country and the flag. Everyone, everywhere yearns for that on some level.

The other hits from that record are enormous too, but so is "Born To Run," which remains some of the best six minutes in rock and roll anywhere, not just on the East Coast of the United States. "The River" can stop the entire stadium in its tracks. It is not surprising if you look at the songs and the lyrics and the stories. Escape and despair are universal; the story of "The River" is as old as dirt, and relevant in any country.

The times in which the crowd came together as one in energy or in reaction or in just pure unadulterated *Oh, my god* always gave me goosebumps, each and every time. There were more of these moments in Europe, or so it seemed, and the emotion and excitement felt larger, stronger, more profound, more communal.

My favorite memories remain the times we were surrounded by fans from every country, speaking every language, with flags and signs and requests and favorite songs, jumping up and down. I adored the nightly sing-along on "The River," loved witnessing the excitement over "Born In The USA," felt part of the unity and excitement on "My Love Will Not Let You Down" or "The Ties That Bind" or even "We Take Care of Our Own," enjoyed throwing myself into the communal fun of "Twist and Shout" and "Seven Nights To Rock," and appreciated the shared awe for "Independence Day" or "Backstreets."

Every night, all around you, people are singing the words as loudly as possible, in every accent imaginable, completely unabashed. Arms in the air punctuate the songs at the same lines you might yourself. There's no thinking that people don't get it or that there's a language barrier or that they somehow don't understand.

It is universal; it is thrilling; it makes you feel at home, no matter what country the land beneath your feet belongs to or what currency you are carrying in your pocket at that moment.

It is astonishing that we can be so united. It is amazing that we are so similar. It is wonderful, every second and every minute of it.

* * *

Seeing Springsteen in Europe absolutely met my expectations, both good and bad. It was such an amazing experience that within days of our return, we are combing through all the rumors and figuring out how we could get back overseas in 2013, when and if the tour continues.

Forget "better"—which is highly subjective anyway—the truth is that the European fan base has become absolutely vital to the sphere of Springsteen fandom. The tours overseas aren't a promotional obligation or a perfunctory gesture (especially when he continues to sell out stadiums everywhere he goes). While many artists with Springsteen's tenure are struggling to find a new audience and remain relevant, in Europe, Bruce has created and maintained a very active and growing audience, which supports him with the kind of fervor and acceptance that the U.S. did in the '80s. With the E Street Band or without it, the European fans are fiercely supportive; while Springsteen struggled to tour with the Seeger Sessions Band in the States, playing less than 20 shows, he was able to play close to 50 concerts in Europe.

As a Springsteen fan, I feel like parts of me belong to both sides of the ocean equally; I resonate with the honest, open gratitude of the fans overseas and prefer their brand of active participation during shows. It is refreshing to be with people who do not take Springsteen for granted. It is astonishing as a fan to watch the differences in the shows as a result. It's especially impossible to ignore the impact of the fan bases in Spain, Italy and Scandinavia; great shows in those countries aren't flukes or accidents, they are just as much of a given as, say, the second show in a two-night stand in Philadelphia.

For me personally, there will never be anything like watching Madison Square Garden come to life singing "Hungry Heart," nothing like the roar of recognition for "Thundercrack" in an old-school Philly crowd, nothing like the shows at Convention Hall in Asbury Park. The goosebumps I get when I walk into MSG or the excitement building on the drive to Philadelphia are practically wired into my DNA.

It would be ridiculous to suggest that the important shows or the great moments only happen in Europe; as I finished this book, Springsteen turned in a legendary show the second night at Fenway Park at the start of the U.S. stadium run, and there are more obscure songs and special moments that still feel like they belong to the Stateside fans. But anyone who stared enviously as the setlists and show reports rolled in from Manchester or Montpelier or Helsinki understands that this is now status quo, not an exception. The European shows give me the opportunity to add new memories and experiences to my list, which is tremendously exciting to me as a fan.

See you on the other side of the pond in 2013.

AN EXCERPT FROM

B-SIDES AND BROKEN HEARTS

A Rock and Roll Novel

By Caryn Rose

B-SIDES AND BROKEN HEARTS - CHAPTER 1: 2001

Joey Ramone is dead.

I cannot believe this, so I read the headline again. PUNK ROCK LEGEND JOEY RAMONE DEAD AT 49.

No. This can't be happening. He's a Ramone. Ramones are comic book characters, eternally youthful, and while, sure, the Ramones had gotten older and broken up, they don't die. Not yet. No.

I sit there, alternately staring into space and rereading the news story, as though I'll see something different the next time I look. I am seized by sadness and anger. I can trace my love of the Ramones back to age fifteen. Twenty-two years? It can't really be twenty-two years, can it? I can't have been in Seattle for over ten years now, right?

The Ramones were simple and outrageous, perfect and anarchic. Elegance in blue jeans, black leather and Converse All-Stars. We all wanted to be that cool. Growing up in a New Jersey full of strip malls and spandex, the Ramones were not just a breath of fresh air, they were nothing short of salvation--just to the right of Chrissie Hynde wearing a red leather jacket and lace fingerless gloves on the cover of the first Pretenders album.

A rapid ding-ding-ding signaling incoming email pulls me out of my reverie. Just like when Johnny Thunders died, the messages pour in and they all say the same thing: "You were one of the first people I thought of when I heard the news." Why does death dissolve all these barriers when life doesn't? It seems sad and wrong.

The Sunday evening silence bears down on me and I suddenly wonder why I'm not listening to anything. I'm about to head over to the CD rack, but then stop myself; if there was ever an analog band, it's the Ramones. So I walk over to the rows and rows of vinyl, pull out all of my Ramones records, and lay them out flat on the floor in chronological order.

I remember buying the first album at Discount Records out on Route 10 and having the sales clerk laugh at me and tell me I should try listening to some real music, that the Ramones sucked, that they could barely play their instruments. I didn't even try to argue, although it was a matter of honor in those days to defend your music to the death. But how could I argue with someone wearing an Emerson, Lake and Palmer t-shirt? It was one of those old 70's rock shirts, black body with white sleeves and a bad bootleg screen print of the cover of Brain Salad Surgery. He had long, stringy hair and John Lennon glasses and I could just tell that he thought he was so cool. Well, he was what passed for cool in the New Jersey suburbs of the late 70's.

Pride of place in my Ramones collection belongs to my autographed End of the Century album, signed by Johnny and Joey in thick black magic marker scrawl, carefully shielded in plastic. In the summer of 1980, there was a record signing down in the Village at that cheap record store on the north side of Eighth Street between Fifth and Sixth. I waited in line for hours and when I approached Joey and Johnny at the signing table, couldn't manage to eke out more than "Hi" and "Thank you." At sixteen, they were larger than life to me, and proximity did nothing to alter that perception.

Later that summer I saw them play live for the first time, one August night at the Dr. Pepper Music Festival, held at Wollman Rink in Central Park. The same year had the Pretenders, the Talking Heads, and the Ramones in one week--punk rock heaven for a girl from the suburbs who had no other chance to see these bands. I snuck into the city after school, walked over from Penn Station to the Korvettes at Herald Square and bought tickets. The prices were five dollars for the floor, three dollars for the balcony. It was all general admission, which meant puke brown metal folding chairs that by the end of the season were rusty and dented from thousands of feet jumping up and down on them night after night.

I still have my photos from that show, taken with a Kodak Instamatic from the tenth row. It was the most amazing thing in the world to actually see the Ramones play. Dee Dee counting down every song "1-2-3-4!" Joey standing there, immovable. Johnny's hands a blur of powerchords on his trademark white Mosrite guitar. I was wearing a red miniskirt, black Converse All-Stars and a plain white boy's t-shirt adorned with carefully chosen rock pins, and entirely too much makeup. I jumped up and down on the rusted metal chairs along with everyone else, and sang along and felt happy and free and at home.

In tribute, I put on the first record, the one with the cover that is still so raw and so revolutionary--Roberta Bayley's black and white portrait of the boys in leather jackets t-shirts, ripped jeans and Converse against a brick wall. At the time, that cover was so unlike anything else out there. Nowadays, it's almost a gold standard. Carrying that album around high school didn't earn me any coolness points, since it wasn't The Wall or the Grateful Dead. It was Punk Rock. Punk Rock was Bad.

I am now childishly determined to get through every single Ramones album I own tonight, in chronological order. I sit forlornly on the floor, hug my knees to my chest like I did when I was fifteen, and stare, mesmerized, at all the album covers. I turn up the volume some more and sing along really loud, memory after memory I have of the Ramones flashing through my brain. I have to get up every twenty minutes to flip the record, and when I do, I stop at the computer to marvel at who else has crawled out of the woodwork after all these years.

I shake myself out of the reverie of reminiscence and wonder who I should call? I should call Marie, because clearly, my best friend, Ms. Punk Rock 1982 of New Brunswick, hasn't heard yet or she would be burning down the phone lines. And I guess I should probably think about dinner, although I have no appetite. Ian is supposed to come over for dinner. I should call and tell him that I really don't feel like eating. Or maybe, maybe we can go out somewhere and drink beer and talk about the Ramones.

I'm formulating my grand Joey Tribute Plans just as the phone rings. Caller ID advertises that it's Ian.

"Hey, I was just about to call you," I say.

"How are you?" he asks.

"Have you seen the news tonight? Joey Ramone is dead, Ian."

"Uh-huh--I mean, really?" Ian says.

"He was forty-nine. Complications from his cancer."

"Wow. That's a bummer," he says, and then continues: "Hey, I got these tomatoes at the Market this afternoon. These are just the best tomatoes I have ever seen. The guy I bought them from grew them himself. He was so proud of his tomatoes that I just had to buy them. I thought I'd make some bruschetta or something Italian with them. They are just so good. You have got to try them."

I take the receiver away from my ear and hold it in my hand, staring at it as though it's a particularly rotten item I just pulled out of the refrigerator. Ian continues to talk, not realizing I wasn't listening. I think of the line in Elvis Costello's song "No Action," where he talks about holding a girl like he would hold something called Bakelite. I remember when I figured out what Elvis was saying in that line. Bakelite was what they used to make telephones out of. I used to think I was so cool for figuring that out. Of course, no one else I knew cared.

All of a sudden there is silence on the other end of the phone.

"Sorry, I was reading some email--I'm hearing from a lot of people I haven't heard from in ages," I say, by way of apology.

"You weren't even listening!" he says. Ian hates it if you are not one hundred percent focused on him at all times. It's worse if he's cranky about something.

"I think it's kind of fair, considering you aren't listening to me either," I say. I was thinking that, but didn't mean to say it out loud.

"I did listen to you!" he says.

I decide to try another approach, since this one is clearly not going to get me anywhere. He must not understand that I'm honestly upset, that Joey was one of us, that it's not just abstract grief over yet another rock and roll death. Ian would want to console me if he knew how sad I felt right now.

"Ian, I'm really bummed about this. I'm sitting here playing all my Ramones records, in order, and remembering. Remember when it used to be dangerous to like the Ramones?" I say this cheerily, as conversationally as I can manage.

"Lisa, I'm sorry you're upset, but--it's not that big of a deal, right? The Ramones had broken up. They were over long before they had broken up. Let's talk about dinner, and I'll come over and cook," he says. I hear him yawning.

"I thought we could go to Hattie's or the Sunset, I'm sure Max would let us hijack the PA, and we can drink cheap beer and pay tribute to Joey," I say.

"It's a Sunday night!" he says.

"I'm not saying let's get drunk and stay out until 2 a.m."

"I'm really tired," he says. "But it was Sunday, so I was looking forward to seeing you. I went shopping today just for dinner."

"We don't lose a Ramone every day."

"Lisa, I'm sorry, yes, it's sad, but--it's not the greatest loss ever endured by the music world that the author of 'Now I Wanna Sniff Some Glue' is no longer with us." He pronounces the song title in artificial, clipped tones.

"That was Dee Dee," I say, automatically. It was like Tourette's or something. I honestly couldn't stop myself.

"What?" he says.

I pause for just a fraction of a second. "That was Dee Dee. Not Joey."

Ian's intake of breath is loud and ragged. Admittedly, I'm deliberately being a stubborn bitch right now, but I could really fucking care less. He's being--well, I don't know what he's being, but this is my ex-lead guitarist rock-and-roll boyfriend and he wants to talk about tomatoes and doesn't care that Joey Ramone is dead.

"Okay, Lisa, you're upset and you're not being rational and I'm not quite sure why, but it's putting a bummer on my Sunday night and I have a hard week ahead of me. Clearly, I don't feel the same way about the Ramones that you do. I was listening to Rush and KISS and my band never played Ramones songs. I just want to make some dinner, watch some TV, and get ready for work tomorrow."

"Listen, Geddy Lee could die and while it wouldn't affect me personally, I could recognize that it was a loss to the music world and would understand why you were organizing a memorial service at Seattle Center." My anger is starting to escape.

"That's not fair and a cheap shot."

"No, it's not a fucking cheap shot. I'm trying to make a point. You love Rush, I can't fucking stand them, but if one of them died I would certainly understand why you would be upset about it and I would be sympathetic toward you and I wouldn't cop the attitude of, 'Well, it isn't like Pete Townshend died or something'."

"Rush is the music of my childhood," he says.

"And the Ramones are the music of my childhood!" I say.

"The difference being that Rush are actually musicians," he says, as though he set up this entire exchange just to get that in there.

I can't believe he just said that. He likes the Ramones just like everyone does, right? I mean, not liking the Ramones is like not liking sex. I suddenly realize that I don't actually know how he feels about them. Right now, this whole conversation is echoing back to the stringy-haired record clerk in New Jersey, and it bothers me. What's more, I don't understand it. This is not Ian talking. Not the Ian I know, anyway.

"Wanna talk about cheap shots?" I say, after a minute.

Now there is a big silence on the other end of the phone. This isn't just about the Ramones or Rush, but I'm not quite sure what it is about. Whatever it is, it's making my stomach hurt.

I dive into the silence. "Ian, this isn't about music or talent or validity. This is about you not fucking getting it." I'm angry. I'm angrier than I should be, actually.

"What am I not getting? The historical importance of the Ramones? I'm sorry, please explain it to me." He's almost hissing in response.

Now, I'm really fucking pissed.

"Listen, asshole. This isn't about who's more valid or who's more talented or if I like the Ramones and you don't. You're not having any respect for my feelings right now." I am so upset my hands are shaking and my voice is unsteady. I can't tell if I'm going to burst into tears at any second or start screaming and throwing things. This is not a normal fight.

"It's hard to respect your feelings when they are completely and totally out of proportion," Ian says. "You're out of control right now. I can't talk to you like this. I think you should go take a bath, watch some TV, go to bed early--"

I didn't hang up. Not really. Hanging up involves violence and drama. I just quietly set the receiver down. The phone was on its way back to the cradle by the time he said the words "watch some TV." I mean, God, I love drowning my sorrows in a night of bad TV as much as the next person, but that was all he seemed to do, and seemed to want to do, lately. I went over there a few weeks ago for dinner and found him engrossed in this documentary on nighttime flora and fauna of the Southwestern desert on the Discovery Channel. I'd had a really bad day at work and wanted a hug and a glass of wine. He actually yelled at me to shut up after I tried to talk to him for the third time. Ian didn't even own a television when we were first dating, and had confessed to having a KILL YOUR TELEVISION bumper sticker on his car just a few years earlier.

The phone rings and I see Ian's number on the display. I sigh and pick it up gingerly.

"What happened? Did you hit the wrong button?" I can hear in his voice that he knows perfectly well that I didn't hit the wrong button, but he's not going to accuse me of anything just yet.

"No, I hung up on you." There, I said it.

"See what I mean? You're just overreacting right now. You're way too emotional over this." He sounds almost triumphant.

"So what if I am? Someone important to me just died," I say, clearly being too emotional.

There is a pause.

"Do you want me to come over and make you dinner or not?" he asks.

For some reason, I decide to be conciliatory. I am thinking that he is angry about something else and if he'd just come over, he could give me a hug and we'd both apologize, make dinner, snuggle up on the couch and watch a movie.

"Ian, c'mon over. We can make dinner and watch a movie, or I can play Ramones records for you and show you photos and tell you stories. I have lots of great Ramones stories," I say as engagingly as I can. I mean it, though.

"No," he says in that annoying petulant voice of his, which I never respond to and generally ignore. "I'm going to wait until you calm down and get more reasonable about this."

"Then you're going to wait a really fucking long time," I say, and this time I really do hang the phone up. Hard. Like in the movies. It didn't make the same clanging bell sound, though. I think you need one of those old phones to do that. The ones made of Bakelite.

The phone rings again. I ignore it, and walk back over to the turntable and flip over End of the Century to side two. "Baby, I Love You" begins to play, in all its glorious Phil Spector over-production. The phone rings and rings, but I put on my headphones, lie down on the floor and close my eyes.

***

What time is it? I must have fallen asleep. I sit up groggily and listen to the wind blowing against the windows. Half-dazed, I look over at the clock; it's almost 11 p.m. I haven't eaten anything, and my head hurts. I struggle to my feet and walk towards the kitchen.

I see that Ian called a few more times after I'd hung up. I should call him, I think. And then, "No. I don't want to call him. I don't care if he's angry. I don't want to talk to him anymore." I'm saying all of this aloud for some reason, and that last line catches at my throat. So I say it again, louder.

"I don't want to talk to him anymore."

Well, that's interesting. It's interesting because it's not exasperated or petulant or annoyed or childish or angry, it's just--flat. It's a statement of fact.

In every relationship I have ever been in, the end never comes in this long drawn out internal debate where I weigh pros and cons and agonize over how I really feel. Or rather, I go through that process but the truth of the matter is, there is a moment, one moment, in which I know it is over. I usually ignore it, deny it, prolong the agony--but that moment is always there.

Maybe it was the night that Ian insisted that we leave the Supersuckers show early for no other reason than he didn't want to be there, despite the fact that I hadn't seen them in eons and Eddie Spaghetti promised to play my favorite song. Maybe it was the night he tried to issue an edict that we weren't going to see Mudhoney because he didn't feel like it, and when I went by myself, he spent the rest of the weekend sulking. (We never missed Mudhoney, ever. We considered Mudhoney a National Treasure that Should Not be Taken For Granted.)

The signs have been there for a while now. I can easily think of other nights, other moments, other conversations where the signal was bad, the connection was broken, and I would look at him like I didn't know who this person was. The moment. You ignore it, because you don't want it to be over.

Right now, I am tired and fed up. I am not filled with love and affection. I don't want to call him and say, this is silly, why are we fighting? I don't care. I feel irritated and resentful and worn out, and I know with perfect certainty that this relationship is over.

I decide to get up and make some soup and read my email. I discover at least a dozen new messages have appeared while I was passed out. I open a can of soup, pour it in a bowl, and stick it in the microwave for three minutes. While it's heating, I scan my inbox. Regina, Jean, Heather--wait, Jake? The microwave beeps that it's finished, and I ignore it.

Jake? I have email from Jake?

Date: Sunday, April 15, 2001
From: jane magazine's #1 bachelor
to: keith richards #1 groupie
subject: gabba gabba hey

hey kid,

Im sure you already heard, tonight we lost joey. we are all bummed out, and you were the first one I thought of. remember when he showed up at our gig at coney island high and we called you screaming and got him to say hi to you on the cell phone? we were all sitting around moping and then christine yelled at us to do something with it. so, mark's writing a song about joey. he went off in a corner and is scribbling frantically. jonathan is ranting that we need to organize a tribute show. scott is just very quiet right now, we're kind of leaving him alone for a bit. me, im just sad.

Its late on Sunday and I dont know if you are still awake but ill be online while we're in here so you can write back too. the fuckers send their love. Christine says, come to la so you can go shopping, and because she misses you. I say come to la so we can get those tattoos we talked about years ago. I found a place on melrose where the clash used to get their tattoos. You know you want to. oh and i miss you too.

Love ya

Jake

I read the email once, twice, three times, feeling like that moment in The Wizard of Oz when Dorothy's world goes from black and white to Technicolor.

I met Jake and his bandmates my first year in Seattle. I'd just moved from Wallingford to this cheap, rundown house in the Central District, which I shared with the sister of someone I worked with. It wasn't fancy, but my roommate was never there, and it was a house and not a studio apartment above a chilly garage.

Jake, Mark, Scott, and Jonathan lived next door. The first time I saw Jake was when he was mowing the lawn with no shirt on. He was incredibly tall, incredibly thin, incredibly pale, and--at the time--had hair down to the middle of his back, looking for all the world like Ian Astbury and Jim Morrison's illegitimate love child. I thought I had died and gone to heaven. (Of course, later everyone would think he looked like Eddie Vedder, but he looked like Eddie when Ed was still pumping gas in San Diego. Ed just managed to get famous before Jake did. It was a sore point with the rock god.)

The first time I talked to Jake was two months later when the four of them had an impromptu band practice--at 3 a.m. I angrily shoved on a pair of Doc Martens over my bare feet, wrapped a hooded sweatshirt around me and went stomping over there, boots unlaced, in a state of high dudgeon. Not generally a good idea in that neighborhood, but I'd seen these guys and I knew they were students or artists or something, and not selling crack out of their kitchen. I stood on their porch, banging on the door, louder and louder and louder until the music stopped.

Jake was the one who opened the door, and greeted me with this adorable puzzled face, gazing down at me. Even at 3 a.m., he was still pretty gorgeous. But I was tired and had to work the next day. Cuteness had no power over me at that moment.

"Hi. I'm your next-door neighbor. I don't know if you were aware, but it's three o'clock in the morning. I love loud rock music as much as the next gal, but it's a school night. Could you turn down the volume?" I yawned up in his direction. I suddenly felt very short.

"Wow, I really like your t-shirt!" Jake said, entirely too brightly for three o'clock in the morning.

What was he talking about? I looked down, not having any memory at that moment of what I was wearing. It was my favorite shirt, a picture of Keith Richards standing in front of a sign reading "A Drug Free America Comes First."

"Did you know that picture was taken in Seattle customs?" he said. "Did you--"

"As it so happens, I was already aware of that," I said, cutting off his overly enthusiastic history lesson. "Could you please turn down the volume on your stereo? Just because it goes to eleven doesn't mean that you have to use all of that wattage."

"It's not the stereo, it's us." He smiled really big. Dimples, too, I noticed, even in my sleep-deprived haze.

Bleary-eyed, I inquired: "Us?"

"Our band! We're called Infinite Trainwreck," he said.

Even half asleep, I could recognize a lousy band name.

"Your band name sucks. I don't know if your music does. But right now I need to sleep. Can you please not practice now." It wasn't a request, it was a demand, and so I didn't even wait to hear his response. I stomped over to my house and went back to bed.

The next day I came home from work and there was an exaggeratedly artistic note duct-taped to the front door and a bouquet of supermarket flowers on the doormat. The note was an invitation to come over and hang out and drink wine. And that was how it all started. They were funny and intelligent, and I loved their music. We became fast friends and stayed that way.

They would later change their name to Blue Electric, get signed to a major label, and move to L.A.--which is a gross oversimplification of the story.

Although I was in terminal denial about it, Ian hated them. Or more specifically, he hated and resented "Jacob" (he always insisted on calling Jake by his proper name), and the feeling was mutual (although Jake constantly denied that, too). Ian didn't speak to me for two weeks when Jake bought me a Rolling Stones record Ian had talked me out of buying, while Jake refused to return my emails for almost a month after Ian mentioned something about us getting married.

"Lisa, he's a fucking jerk. He's old and sad and bitter that his band didn't hit it big, and he's devoting his entire life to making everyone else miserable for that reason," Jake said over the phone, after I threatened to get on a plane and find him in L.A. if he didn't start talking to me.

"Yes, but I soften him up," I said.

"Yeah, as long as you do what he wants you to, when he wants you to."

"Jake, that is so unfair and not true. I came down to L.A. to the opening show of the last tour, even though Ian couldn't go because of work."

"And he was crabby about it for like six weeks, wasn't he?"

I had no retort to that statement, because Jake was right.

The phone rings again. It's Ian. This time, I pick it up.

"Where have you been? I've been calling all night," he says.

"I fell asleep on the floor with headphones on," I say. I have no energy to be pissed off. But then, it occurs to me that he might actually have been worried. He would go through phases at work when a case in the criminal division would disturb him so much he would check on me constantly, not telling me anything more than there were still fucked up people out there, and reminding me that the police still hadn't caught Mia Zapata's killer.

"I was calling to see if you were ready to apologize," he says.

Well, I guess he wasn't that worried.

Seconds tick by while I hold back my immediate reaction, which is to tell him to go fuck himself and hang up again. More seconds tick by, and yet more seconds. And then I realize that this is pointless, I have nothing to say to him, and he won't hear me anyway.

So I hang the phone up, quietly this time, and unplug it from the wall so I can't hear it ring if he calls back, which I don't think he will. I sit down, open up a new email message, and type:

to: i am a rock god!
from: lisa
subject: joey ramone is dead.

jake. i'm freaked. joey is dead. how did this happen? he's a ramone. ramones don't die.

it's raining (shocker, i know). i have a headache. i just realized that my boyfriend is an asshole and there's no way i can possibly marry this guy. he doesn't care joey is dead.

I would love to come to L.A.. Tell me what your schedule is. and give everyone a hug from me. tell scott that he has to stop buying me sonic youth singles!

xoxo

--l.

I hit send and then start answering the deluge of email prompted by Joey's death. There are so many memories and so many people I miss sitting in my inbox. Leaving New York was such a hard thing, but I had to do it or I would have probably gone mad, killed myself, or both. Too many people I know did burn out, including some of the people whose names are in front of me right now. But these are the ones who made it through to the other side. I watched people I loved crash and burn, burn until there was nothing left. And then I ended up being an innocent bystander at what was probably the worst kind of hit and run destruction of a life, ever. All for the love of rock and roll, like the song says. Stupid kids thinking they will play guitar just like Keith Richards if they mimic everything about him.

It seems so long ago that I woke up in the East Village one morning and decided to move to Seattle. It was the best thing I have ever done.

I am still busily replying to messages when a response from Jake arrives with a loud DING.

Date: Sunday, April 15, 2001
From: I wanna be your monkeywrench
to: standing in the shadows
subject: going to california

what are you waiting for? Im not going anywhere. the new house has plenty of room, and girlfriend #87 is no longer on the scene. Do you need a ticket? Call the office tomorrow morning and its yours. But call me and let me have your plane info so I can pick you up myself. Much love

the rock god

p.s. why did you have to go and date a fucking yuppie wannabe loser so you couldn't come and hang out with us any more? good riddance. christine agrees. he didn't even have any money to redeem himself, and he listens to fucking dave matthews. you hate dave matthews.

Jake was right. That should have been the ultimate sign that something was very wrong: Ian had started listening to Dave Matthews.

Dave fucking Matthews was the Antichrist. He was the anti-everything I--we (or so I thought)--cared about in music.

Ian hid the CDs from me and certainly never listened to them when I was around. I only found out about this secret passion (it wasn't even a guilty pleasure, much to my dismay) when I ran into his friend Greg at Larry's Market one night and he asked me if I was coming with them to see DMB at the Gorge.

I looked at him like he was speaking another language.

"Greg. We don't listen to Dave Matthews," I said. "We're the people who drive 300 miles in one night to see Sonic Youth."

"Maybe you don't, Lisa, but Ian bought the tickets and it was his idea."

"No way. This has got to be some kind of perverse practical joke."

"We're even camping overnight at the Gorge!"

"Oh, brother. Well, maybe Ian forgot to tell me," I said, thinking that he had to be doing this as some kind of male bonding thing with his friends. Surely he could not be serious about this.

He was.

"What's wrong with Dave Matthews? I'll have you know, he is an excellent guitar player. Have you ever really listened to any of their records?" Ian said.

I couldn't fault him for being a little bit pissed off, given that I'd spent the day sending him e-cards of Dave Matthews every few hours. That would have been okay, but then I had to ask him if this meant he would wear Dockers and polar fleece out to the Cha-Cha Lounge. He stormed out the door and didn't talk to me for three days.

That's when I knew that this wasn't a guilty pleasure. Oh, well. I just thought it was a minor aberration; you're not always going to have 100% musical compatibility.

(But--*Dave Matthews*?)

That's it, I decide: I am going to L.A.. I've deprived myself of my friends for too long. I'm perusing flight schedules online when it dawns on me: I can wait until tomorrow and get on a plane or I can throw everything in the car and leave now.

I have always wanted to drive to California, but for some reason it just never happened. Roadtripping wasn't that easy in the Northwest; once you hit Portland, the next major city is San Francisco, twelve hours later. And, well, life is a little different now.

But like any good Jersey girl, I loved to drive. I loved driving alone, watching the trucks zoom by at night, marker lights blinking like Christmas trees. I loved driving with friends, singing along to bad, tinny Top 40 AM stations, buying tacky souvenirs at truck stops. Driving home from Philadelphia or D.C. and waking up at the same point on the New Jersey Turnpike, where the lights on the refinery turned it into an Emerald City. Staring at the radio relay towers blinking red in the distance and wanting to follow them forever.

I close my eyes and I can see it. I can feel the car moving. I can hear the radio playing and my friends talking, and the yearning for that feeling of freedom hurts somewhere inside the center of my chest.

First things first: I find an old army knapsack in the closet and grab CDs by the handful. Afghan Whigs, always good for bitter tales of lost love. My Springsteen bootlegs, no question. My beloved Rolling Stones, as if I could go anywhere without them. The Who, *Badmotorfinger* by Soundgarden, Motown compilations for that goofy thing you can sing along to by heart in the middle of the night when you're falling asleep despite gallons of fast food coffee. R.E.M. catches my eye; I think of *Reckoning*, and the summer of listening to that album on repeat while a carload of us drove around the East Coast to show after show. The first three Cheap Trick albums and *Live At Budoka*n. Elvis Costello. The entire X catalog, mandatory for a trip to Los Angeles. Gram Parsons, Uncle Tupelo, Dylan. The Bowie box set, *London Calling* and *Sandinista*, Lou and the Velvets, Neil Young. I'm not consciously looking for roadtrip music; it's more like inviting friends to keep me company along the way.

And then I pause and carefully, reverentially, pull out the two Ramones CDs I own, *All The Stuff And More, Volumes I and II*. That might not sound like a lot, but being the Ramones, two CDs means I have over sixty songs.

Next, I grab a duffel bag and walk into the bedroom. There's no logic, just happy, free-association packing. This is about favorite clothes, cool clothes, rock chick clothes, all the black clothes that looked so good with my blonde hair but were wasted up here in the land of Birkenstocks and flannel shirts. Finally, I am going to get a chance to wear everything I barely have a reason to. Low-cut jeans, blue and black. Underwear--and I'm gleefully digging the good stuff out of the back of the drawer. I don't think for a minute that anyone but me will ever see it, but that's a good enough reason. Shoes break down into two categories, Converse All-Stars and boots, and I add my sad and lonely pair of high heels for good measure.

I finish getting ready in twenty minutes, exactly. This seems much easier than it should be and I am terrified that I am forgetting something. "Maps are in the car. Phone charger is in the car. Bottle of water is in the car. Sleeping bag is in the trunk..." I recite the list like a mantra to keep me safe, or more likely, make me brave enough to go through with this.

The last thing I need to do is email my manager and claim a family emergency. I deliberately do not change my voicemail, because I don't need Ian calling me at work in the morning and have my message inform him that I am going to be gone for a week or two.

That final business detail complete, I sit back in my desk chair, and take a deep breath. My cheeks are flushed with excitement. I take another deep breath and push my bangs out of my face. There's an air of finality, mixed with a slight tinge of danger, settling about me that I kind of like. Is it finality or resignation? No, it feels more like rebellion. I'm going, dammit. I'm just going.

Balancing bags, I grab the doorknob, take one last deep breath to settle myself, and walk out of the apartment. Outside, it is dark and cool and quiet, that deep, Sunday-night-12:00 a.m. kind of quiet.

Key in the ignition, I start the car, and then slide the faceplate into the stereo, watching the equalizer come to life and illuminate the interior of the car in soft greens and blues. For the life of me, I have no idea what I want to listen to first. I sit, letting the engine run for a while, hands gripping the steering wheel for dear life. It feels like I don't know where I'm going.

And then it hits me--I smile and take the Replacements out of the knapsack, cue the disc up to "Someone Take The Wheel." As I pull onto I-5 in the deep Sunday night blackness, I sing along with pseudo-ebullience; I mean it but I don't quite feel it yet, and I'm hoping that throwing myself into the spirit of the moment will bring me around. I am seized by confusion, I am bursting with excitement, and I am plain old borderline terrified. But I am absolutely bound and fucking determined to face it all head-on for the first time in ages.

Thirty minutes later, I am passing through Tacoma. While I still have this odd raw terror and irrational fear of the unknown churning around my stomach, I feel a lot better, and settle into the rhythm of driving. Fort Lewis. Nisqually Basin. The first sign for the Sleater-Kinney Road exit heralding Olympia. I consider stopping at the next rest stop for coffee, but I'm afraid that if I stop moving I'll be seized by reality, change my mind, turn around, and go back home.

What am I so scared of? I do this all the time--or rather, I used to do this. What is this big gaping hole in my chest? Since when did I get so scared of--well, I don't know what I'm scared of. But I am going to keep driving, and maybe I'll find out.

* * *

Enjoyed this book?

B-sides and Broken Hearts is available worldwide in paperback and ebook:

Amazon.com

Barnes and Noble

Indiebound

iBookstore

More information:

bsidesandbrokenhearts.com

ABOUT THE AUTHOR

Caryn Rose is a Brooklyn-based writer and novelist who documents rock and roll, baseball and urban life. She has been writing about Bruce Springsteen for over 30 years, and has been a regular contributor to *Backstreets* Magazine since 2003. Her first novel, *B-sides and Broken Hearts*, was published in 2011, and her second novel, *You Can't Predict Baseball*, is slated for release in the Spring of 2013. *Raise Your Hand: Adventures of an American Springsteen Fan In Europe* is her first non-fiction book. You can follow her online at jukeboxgraduate.com or on Twitter @carynrose.

18677262R00080

Made in the USA
Lexington, KY
19 November 2012